Also available at all good book stores

9781785318641

9781785316470

9781801500067

9781785318627

9781801500562

9781801501101

9781785313233

9781785315749

9781801500906

BRAWLS, BRIBES AND

BROKEN
DREAMS

BRAWLS, BRIBES AND

BROKEN DREAMS

How Dundee Almost
Won the European Cup

Graeme Strachan

First published by Pitch Publishing, 2022

Pitch Publishing
9 Donnington Park,
85 Birdham Road,
Chichester,
West Sussex,
PO20 7AJ
www.pitchpublishing.co.uk
info@pitchpublishing.co.uk

A CIP catalogue record is available for this book
from the British Library.

ISBN 978 1 80150 101 9

Typesetting and origination by Pitch Publishing
Printed and bound in India by Replika Press Pvt. Ltd.

Contents

For Esmée and Lewis

Acknowledgements

THANKS TO Jane Camillin at Pitch for believing in the project and Duncan Olner for the cover design which brings that special period to life in glorious colour.

Llew Walker set the ball rolling while David Powell, Barry Sullivan and Gary Thomas from the DC Thomson archives team have been of great assistance throughout. David Lord has been hugely supportive and a big thanks to Patrick Barclay for sprinkling his magic dust and taking us down memory lane with his foreword.

A special mention also to Ruth, Rachel, Esmée and Lewis, who have kept the home fires burning while I pounded the laptop at ungodly hours of the day and night!

Finally, my heartfelt thanks to Norrie Price, who played the Bob Shankly role, and whose help and guidance throughout has been above and beyond the call of duty.

Foreword

By Patrick Barclay

I WAS delighted to be asked to write the foreword to Graeme's latest book *Brawls, Bribes and Broken Dreams: How Dundee Almost Won the European Cup*.

That was an era that remains close to my heart and I know that to be the case for many others also. It brings back so many wonderful memories – they never actually went away – of our youth, the city of Dundee as it was then and of course that wonderful Dundee FC team of the early 1960s.

I went on to write about the game professionally and was privileged to enjoy glamorous trips to far-off places in Europe and indeed across the world. This involved covering games in the Champions League, successor of course to the European Cup, World Cups, European Championships and even the Africa Cup of Nations.

None of that, though, gave me as much joy as that Dundee team did between 1961 and 1964.

The club had enjoyed great days before, most recently the two League Cup wins featuring the great Billy Steel in 1951 and 1952. My grandfather used to tell me about the players in the 1910 Scottish Cup-winning team and I badgered him to take me to Dens Park. It was the mid-50s when he finally relented and although he, himself, was no longer keen on attending, he dropped me off behind the main stand with a shilling in my pocket for admission.

I think we beat Hibs that night but it was a rocky period of transition for the club under Willie Thornton. He had, though, signed several talented youngsters and his successor Bob Shankly then blended these players with the experience of Bobby Seith, Bobby Wishart and the great Gordon Smith, whose classy displays were to bely his age.

Smith provided glamour. This was a guy who would holiday in Cannes and had a taste for jazz. He became a close friend of Sidney Bechet and even had dinner with Brigitte Bardot. Smith not only mixed with film stars but he looked the part and here he was in Dundee!

They were all heroes but like thousands of others my favourite player was Alan Gilzean, whom I idolised. I was there at Muirton Park as a 14-year-old when Dundee won the league and was amongst the thousands who invaded the pitch. I'd travelled on one of the supporters' buses but inevitably the crowded, joyous road back to Dundee meant I was late for my paper round which on Saturday evenings mainly meant delivering the *Sporting Post*.

The newsagent, however, merely gave me a kindly shake of his head and that night the customers were every bit as understanding! For us back then, this was simply our Dark Blue heaven! Now it was on to the European Cup. Along with a couple of pals, I was in the Provie Road end for the initial tie against Cologne holding aloft my home-made banner which my mum had helped me put together.

On an incredible night, Dundee scored five times before half-time and my flag disappeared into the ecstatic crowd. This was to be a European journey like no other. There was an abundance of goals, violence on and off the field, bumper Dens Park attendances, allegations of bribery – all to a background of the worst winter in living memory.

History will tell that Dundee fell short at the penultimate stage, as had other British clubs like Hibs, Rangers, Tottenham Hotspur and Manchester United before them. Had they reached Wembley, I believe that they would have gone on to win the European Cup. And had they done so might we also have held on to our top stars like Ian Ure and Alan Gilzean – and gone on to further successes?

We will never know but what I can say is that this irrepressible team were happy together. They were exceptional people, they were exceptional players. The one downside was that we, the fans of that era, were spoiled for we would never quite see their like again. How a provincial club like Dundee almost won the European Cup makes fascinating reading and has catapulted me back in time. I hope you also enjoy this fabulous trip down memory lane.

Prologue

*'If we win the league on Saturday you'll be
famous forever more.'*

Gordon Smith

IT WAS a glorious summer back in 1962.

Dundee FC had just been crowned champions of
Scotland for the first time and qualified for the European
Cup, later to develop into the Champions League.

Young boys played football in the streets and parks
of Dundee, imagining themselves as their very own
heroes in dark blue.

The championship success had brought a feelgood
factor to the city, the centre of jute, jam and journalism
with a population of 180,000.

This was a Dundee side that would never be
forgotten.

Author, broadcaster and authority on Scottish football Bob Crampsey declared that Bob Shankly's Dundee FC in the early 1960s were better than Jock Stein's Lisbon Lions and 'the best pure footballing team produced in Scotland since the war'.

Indeed, now – even 60 years on – that heroic Dundee XI of Liney, Hamilton, Cox, Seith, Ure, Wishart, Smith, Penman, Cousin, Gilzean and Robertson still trips off the tongue of every Dens Park fan.

George McGeachie, Bobby Waddell, Alex Stuart and Craig Brown made up the squad of 15 and all played their part.

But that famous XI missed so few games during the 1961/62 season that it was they alone who became known as the Dundee FC league-winning team.

Previously, the club had won the Scottish Cup in 1910 and more recently League Cups in 1951 and 1952, but this was by far the pinnacle of their achievements.

Shankly had prepared them with a summer tour of Iceland that cemented an enduring bond and Dundee began their 1961/62 league campaign with two wins and a defeat before going on a thrilling 19-game unbeaten run which included a double over Celtic and Rangers in early November.

First they dumped Celtic 2-1 with goals from Bobby Wishart and Alan Gilzean before Rangers were taken apart 5-1 in a blanket of fog with Gilzean scoring four.

Goalkeeper Pat Liney famously had to ask right-back Alex Hamilton what the score was because he couldn't see the Rangers goal area.

That left Dundee seven points clear of the champions, but there were other highlights galore.

There were high-scoring wins over Kilmarnock 5-3, Motherwell 4-2 and Raith Rovers 5-4.

There was home and away success over the Edinburgh pair of Hearts and Hibs.

Opponents were adjusting, though.

They were figuring out ways to cut off the supply line from talented winger Gordon Smith and slow Dundee down.

A shock Scottish Cup exit to St Mirren at the end of January was followed by a worrying loss of league form which brought just one draw for their next five games.

It was an ill-timed dose of the wintertime blues but in mid-March came the high-noon moment with the midweek visit of league leaders Rangers.

Billed as a 'winner-takes-all' confrontation, the result was a no-score draw on a tension-ridden night before 35,000 fans at Dens.

But although the Ibrox men remained three points ahead, Dundee's battling performance had restored their flagging belief.

Indeed, they proceeded to win their next five matches with Liney highlighting a gift of a good luck charm as a possible reason for their change in fortune.

A woman and her daughter gave Liney a piece of dried meat from a River Tay seal with dark blue ribbons wrapped around it.

Liney took it on to the park for his next game and put it in the net behind him.

On 31 March 1962, with five games remaining, Bob Miller of the *People's Journal* declared: 'Dundee should hammer the lot – except maybe (Dundee) United.' Stirling Albion and Airdrie were defeated.

But although Dundee had won the earlier derby 4-1 at Dens, the Easter Monday clash at Tannadice was a tighter game which they edged 2-1 thanks to a last-minute goal by Gilzean.

The title race went down to the wire.

Dundee and Rangers were now level on points with two games to go.

Dundee played St Mirren at home while Rangers were away to Aberdeen.

Alan Cousin put Dundee in front before St Mirren got a penalty with 12 minutes to go.

Centre-half Jim Clunie stepped up from 12 yards to take the spot kick.

Liney's father was a St Mirren fan and when the sides met in the Scottish Cup in January he told his son that Clunie would go for the top-right corner if they got a penalty.

He remembered his father's advice and got a hand to it when Clunie took his kick.

Liney smothered the ball when he landed.

Andy Penman went up the park almost immediately and made it 2-0.

The public address system crackled into life at full time and the stadium announcer's voice was lost in a great roar as he read out the result from Pittodrie.

Aberdeen had defeated Rangers 1-0 and police had to force their way through the crowd to rescue Liney from the jubilant fans who streamed on to the pitch to celebrate.

Gordon Smith came up to Liney after the game and told him, 'People will remember that forever. If we win the league on Saturday you'll be famous forever more.'

Dundee now just needed a point in their final game against St Johnstone to win the title.

A vast army of 20,000 Dundee supporters made it through to Perth on trains, cars and buses to see the league clinched for the first time in the club's 69-year history.

Two special trains left from Dundee West Station at 1.40pm and 1.50pm, both packed to the rafters, the 2pm normal service picked up the stragglers.

Most of the fans going by car and bus left at lunchtime and there were 700 vehicles an hour passing through Longforgan by 2pm.

Thirteen years earlier, Dundee squandered their opportunity of lifting the title with defeat at Falkirk as Rangers overcame Albion Rovers to win by a point.

But this time they were to hold their nerve against a St Johnstone side which included a young Alex Ferguson in their ranks.

Saints were in good form and they needed a point to avoid relegation.

Back in those days there was little protection from the hatchet men.

Gordon Smith was targeted and suffered a leg injury which was heavily bandaged before Dundee's supremacy began to show in front of 26,500 at Muirton Park.

For 25 minutes things were in the balance but two goals from Alan Gilzean and one from Andy Penman gave Dundee a 3-0 victory which also relegated Saints to the second tier, along with Stirling Albion.

Jubilant Dundee fans jumped the fence and invaded the pitch to celebrate on the final whistle and skipper Bobby Cox was lifted shoulder-high by the masses.

The supporters sang and danced and chanted and some of the Dundee players eventually ventured into the main stand to receive further plaudits.

'It's Dundee's League' was the *Sporting Post* headline on Saturday evening. Cox described the title success as his greatest moment in football.

The captain and his team-mates travelled home from Perth on the team bus along the old A92.

The celebrations were already in full swing back in Dundee where 5,000 fans had assembled in the City Square and swamped the surrounding streets.

Dundee's team bus was given a police escort to the City Square where Cox was the first to get off with his arms in the air after leaving Muirton Park with the match ball.

The players and officials managed to navigate the steps to take a bow from the tiny balcony of the City Chambers and the party was now in full flow.

The JM Ballroom was chock-a-block, as were all the pubs.

Dundee's players and officials had drinks at chairman James Gellatly's home after the ceremony before going out to party together.

Manager Shankly returned home to bed but was woken at 12.30am by a Dundee man in New York who heard the news of the title win at 7pm on Broadway.

He had spent hours obtaining Shankly's home number before calling from across the Atlantic to offer his congratulations.

All part and parcel of being a successful manager perhaps, but, in a return to domestic normality, Shankly was pictured mowing his lawn the following day!

Later the Dundee boss would describe how he had to go through a huge batch of congratulatory letters, telegrams, postcards, cablegrams and messages which had arrived at Dens.

He said, 'It's great how folk come to the surface again at a time like this.

'I got a wee catch in my throat when I opened letters from a couple of men I hadn't seen for 30 years.

'One bloke said it all in verse while another said this is easily the best team that has ever worn the colours.

'Well, he could be right!'

The significance of Dundee's domestic achievement was brought home just days later when Benfica and Real Madrid contested the European Cup Final in Amsterdam.

They were the only two clubs that had won the competition since its inception in 1955.

Eusébio scored a double in a 5-3 win for the Portuguese champions as Benfica went on to lift the famous trophy for a second consecutive year.

Eusébio was Europe's new superstar and poster boy, outshone on the global stage only by Pelé, whose Brazil side were the new big boys of world football.

This was the glamorous new world which Dundee now found themselves in.

The draw for the European Cup would be made in July. Dundee, meanwhile, would participate in the American International Soccer League from 20 May to 17 June.

The ISL was the first modern attempt to create a major soccer league in the US and featured guest teams, primarily from Europe but also Mexico, South America, Canada and Asia.

The New York tournament would provide the perfect preparation for the European Cup against sides from West Germany, Brazil, Yugoslavia, Mexico and Italy.

The players got a tremendous send-off from an enthusiastic crowd of 1,000 supporters who crammed the platform at Dundee West Station to wish them good luck.

Shankly, trainer Sammy Kean and physio Lawrie Smith were the backroom team who had done so much to orchestrate the team's success.

Shankly said, 'I'm sure we'll enjoy ourselves, but let's face it – a team cannot really enjoy a trip like this unless it's a winning one.

'We are going out to win. That comes first.'

Dundee were staying at Hotel Empire on Broadway on 63rd Street and on their first night several players went to watch a heavyweight boxing fight at St Nicholas Arena.

Billy Daniels, a hot fighter on a 16-bout winning streak, was defeated in round seven by a young man named Cassius Clay, who would later go by the name of Muhammad Ali.

The players got to meet Clay after the fight and the following day Dundee played against West German side Reutlingen in the first match of the tournament.

The ISL consisted of two groups of six. Dundee struggled to cope with the heat and humidity in their opening game on Randall's Island.

The game drew 17,444 fans which was a record for an opening-day game on what was New York's hottest afternoon for more than half a century.

The weather was so hot that 37-year-old winger Smith was taken to hospital with severe dehydration after losing over a stone in weight.

Dundee flew to Detroit afterwards to play a friendly game against another West German side, Saarbrücken, where they went down 5-1 at the Tiger Stadium.

Dundee then returned to tournament action in New York, where a 3-3 draw against Hajduk Split of

Yugoslavia was followed by a 3-2 win over Guadalajara of Mexico.

Smith was given a chance to escape the stifling heat and flew home after the victory.

Dundee finished second from bottom of the group after a 1-1 draw with Palermo from Italy then a 3-2 defeat by América-RJ from Brazil, who went on to win the tournament.

Dundee were beaten by the heat and were given a lesson in possession football.

The trip would prove critical for the forthcoming European Cup campaign and convinced manager Shankly to put in place a new counter-attacking style.

At that time the 1962 World Cup finals were taking place in Chile. Scotland had missed out on qualification despite an abundance of talent at their disposal.

Czechoslovakia finished as runners-up to Brazil while the Scotland players they beat in a qualifying play-off in Brussels remained at home.

In the absence of the injured Pelé, Garrincha would guide Brazil to victory against a Czechoslovakia side whose captain Josef Masopust was named European Footballer of the Year in 1962. Masopust played for Dukla Prague who were among the favourites for the

European Cup, which would start in September with Dundee amongst the 30 teams taking part.

AC Milan, Benfica and the five-time winners Real Madrid were at the peak of their powers while Ipswich Town – the shock underdogs who had come good just like Dundee – would represent England after winning the league under Alf Ramsey.

The hopes for Dundee weren't as lofty, but strange things can happen in football.

The Scottish champions were relatively small fry but they were to embark on an incredible fairy-tale run which took them tantalisingly close to the European Cup Final at Wembley and the opportunity of becoming the first British side to win that much-coveted trophy.

This is Dundee's story.

Chapter 1

The Other Shankly

'We have no delusions, no ideas, that we
are on an easy thing.'

Dundee chairman James Gellatly

DUNDEE WOULD become the fourth side to represent Scotland in the European Cup.

The club that led British football into European competition was Edinburgh's Hibernian in 1955 after reigning Scottish champions Aberdeen declined the invite.

Willie Thornton was Dundee manager when Hibs reached the inaugural semi-finals in 1955/56 and he was already laying the foundations that would lead to future success. The former Rangers star had assembled a good side at Dens Park since arriving in 1954.

Young players were being given their chance including Pat Liney, Alex Hamilton, Bobby Cox, Ian Ure, George McGeachie, Andy Penman, Alan Cousin, Alan Gilzean and Hugh Robertson.

Thornton, however, resigned in October 1959 for 'family reasons' and returned to Glasgow to become manager of Partick Thistle.

He had achieved a credible fourth-place finish for Dundee the season before.

That, though, had been somewhat overshadowed by a shock Scottish Cup first-round loss to Highland League part-timers Fraserburgh.

Dundee's form that season had been indifferent and particularly poor at home, and there was a feeling Thornton had taken the club as far as he could.

The club advertised the job and Bob Shankly duly answered the call.

Shankly came to Dens Park after previously managing Falkirk and Third Lanark.

Another applicant was his brother Bill, then managing Huddersfield Town.

Bill's letter arrived the day after his older brother had already been appointed.

The rest is history.

Bill went on to take the Liverpool job in December and few would disagree that it was he who helped transform the sleeping giant into the great club it is now.

His older brother in Dundee became a managerial mentor during those early years at Liverpool and they talked on the phone every Monday evening about football.

On the same day as Dundee's title win, Bill's Anfield Reds won the Second Division title and promotion to the top flight in England, which made it a league double for the Shankly brothers.

Bob Shankly was to make some shrewd signings at Dens to build on the solid foundations which had already been established by Thornton.

These included bringing in English title-winner Bobby Seith, who had been training with Dundee during the summer of 1960 after leaving Burnley.

The powerful right-half had helped the Clarets win the First Division but a disagreement with chairman Bob Lord ended with him handing in a transfer request.

The transfer fee paid by Shankly was to prove a £7,500 bargain as Seith brought with him priceless experience and big-game knowledge.

The man from Monifieth added to a solid core of the three Cs of Bobby Cox, Doug Cowie and Alan Cousin. Seith was soon seen as a driving force.

For his part, Bobby Cox was a Dundee boy who had been born just a few hundred yards from Dens.

Cox had replaced the legendary Cowie as club captain in the summer of 1961 after Shankly decided to release the veteran left-half.

The inspirational left-back Cox is often remembered as a terrier in the tackle but he was a very fine footballer and quite simply the heart and soul of the team.

In January 1961, Shankly secured inside-left Bobby Wishart, who had previously won the league with Aberdeen in 1955, and shrewdly dropped him back to left-half.

But his masterstroke was the signing of 37-year-old Gordon Smith, who had been pensioned off by Hearts in the summer of 1961 following a recurring ankle injury.

Smith was known as Scotland's Stanley Matthews and was part of the 'Famous Five' forward line that helped steer Hibs to three league titles in the 1940s and 1950s. Prior to that the Montrose man had turned out for Dundee North End juniors, but the presence of his friend and ex-Easter Road team-mate Sammy Kean was a key factor in him signing.

A lover of fast cars who turned up for his first day at Dens in a Porsche, film addict Smith was just as big an idol for a generation of post-war football fans.

The man with the movie star looks had even appeared as an extra in Alfred Hitchcock's movie *To Catch a Thief* in 1954 when he was in Cannes for an 18-day break.

He also won the league with Hearts after being released by Hibs and was the only player from the Dundee squad to have gained experience in the European Cup.

He had done so with both Edinburgh clubs, making a semi-final appearance for Hibs in 1955/56, and had been capped 18 times by Scotland.

Albeit a veteran, his arrival was something akin to royalty.

Bobby Seith said, 'The first time he played with us was on a pre-season tour of Iceland and at the end of it he pulled me aside and said this team could win the championship.

'When Gordon said something like that, he wasn't being light-hearted about it.'

Smith, of course, was correct, and was a hugely influential figure in Dundee's championship success as he achieved the unique distinction of being the only player to win the league with three different teams.

The fact none of those teams were Celtic or Rangers made it all the more remarkable.

Edinburgh-based Smith trained at home for most of the week because he combined football with business, running his post office and a pub called the Right Wing.

The signing of Smith had not been universally acclaimed by the fans, as Shankly explained.

'What a tanking I took when I signed him,' he said.

'He was too old, too anxious to steer clear of injury, etc.

'But he was just the man I wanted.

'A man who can read a game and play accordingly; who is always in the place other players expect him to be and can put the brake on the side if need be.

'When the fans saw how astute Gordon was and how much stemmed from him, they understood what he brought and forgave his reduced speed.'

Dundee played what was termed as 'simple football with no gimmicks' with a trick or two, as well as a blend of pace and guile and a measure of tactical consciousness.

For a good number of years, Dundee had been known as the 'Dapper Dans' of Scottish football. This was because their short passing style was in contrast to the more direct approach adopted by many of their opponents in Scotland.

In recent times, this had seen them climb to fourth place in 1958/59 and 1959/60, while there had also been an impressive high-scoring run in 1960/61 until leg breaks suffered by Andy Penman and George McGeachie. Too often recognised as having a soft centre, the emergence of the combative Ian Ure at centre-half had gone far to allay that accusation.

Smith and Hugh Robertson provided the ammunition for the prolific Alan Gilzean, who was partnered up front by Alan Cousin, the catalyst for many attacks with his thrusting runs from deep. The leggy Cousin had mastered the art of the 'double shuffle' which effectively saw him slow down then, with a deft shuffle of his feet and change of pace, accelerate past his bewildered opponents.

People used to ask him about the double shuffle. Cousin would tell them that he had no idea how it came about. He said he did it one time and it seemed to work so he carried on doing it.

Always good for a goal and top scorer for three seasons until 1960, Cousin was held in high regard by his team-mates for his great work rate, often tracking back to help out his defence.

Cousin was part-time and combined football with studies in Greek and Latin at St Andrews University, and thereafter became a languages teacher in his home town of Alloa.

One persistent mystery was the presence of goalkeeper Sandy Davie in one of Dundee's team photographs which was taken at their 1961/62 pre-season public trial match.

Davie went on to have a successful career with Dundee United but along with his father, he had grown up a Dundee supporter. He was a huge fan of goalkeeper Bill Brown, who was a member of Dundee's 1951 League Cup-winning side, and had even bought his first pair of football boots in Dens star Billy Steel's sports shop.

Davie was wanted by both city clubs. But with 17-year-old Ally Donaldson signed as reserve for Pat Liney and Shankly wanting to send Davie to a junior side for experience, Davie opted for Tannadice, where he got an early opportunity.

Donaldson, who was in another group picture at that public trial, had to wait longer for his first-team breakthrough but became just as popular a figure at Dens Park where he spent a total of 16 years, making over 400 appearances, the fifth-highest by a Dundee player. In addition to Liney, the tall Edinburgh teenager had been the only back-up goalkeeper in 1961/62 until the experienced Les Cameron was brought in as support.

An abortive attempt had been made by Shankly in January 1962 to sign Bert Slater from Liverpool, but now Shankly wanted to strengthen ahead of the European Cup.

Shankly had rated Slater highly ever since he was his manager at Falkirk.

He had given Slater his Brockville debut and the goalkeeper was part of the Falkirk side which won the 1957 Scottish Cup after Shankly left for Third Lanark.

Two years after that, Slater signed for Liverpool and played against Dundee in a game to mark the installation of the Dens floodlights in March 1960.

Slater was impressive for Liverpool, despite scoring an own goal when he stepped back over the line after catching a Hugh Robertson corner.

Yet he would later be replaced by James Furnell and told he had no future at Liverpool despite wanting to stay and fight for his place.

That was made clear when Bill Shankly named six goalkeepers ahead of him in the pecking order, right down to the under-12 goalkeeper.

Bob Shankly finally got his man when Slater signed for £2,500 in summer 1962.

Shankly had also recruited 19-year-old Doug Houston from Queen's Park after another winger, Ronnie Crichton, and centre-halves Billy McMillan and Billy Smith were released.

Arbroath man Smith was seen to be unlucky after sustaining an injury in a League Cup tie against Rangers in 1960.

That had seen Ian Ure moving to centre-half and the big fair-haired defender had never looked back.

Slater joined up with the squad following the New York tournament to find the city of Dundee struck by a deadly polio epidemic with new cases appearing at the rate of one per day.

The epidemic centred on Fintry but affected Douglas and Maryfield as it spread and claimed the life of 38-year-old George Craigie from Fintry Mains.

Within days of the alarm being raised, 75,000 people had queued for a sugar lump coated with the vaccine and there was genuine panic in the city.

The health department embarked on an exhaustive campaign and 179,000 people were eventually vaccinated across Dundee.

The outbreak had effectively fizzled out by July before the European Cup draw paired Dundee with West German champions Cologne in the preliminary round.

Back at Dens, the official photographs of Dundee's championship-winning squad had revealed that the team would play in a new crew-necked dark blue and white strip in the forthcoming 1962/63 season.

This was the first change in style since switching from the rugby-collar type to the famous V-necked version in 1956. It was so popular that local sports shops like David Low Sports in the Seagate and Meldrum Sports in Reform Street were unable to keep up with demand for replicas.

Peter Black's 'Football Know-All and Pools Guide' was published in the *Weekly News* and appeared to write off Dundee's chances of European success.

The form guide was printed over two weeks every year prior to the start of the season with complete details of all 37 senior clubs as well as an assessment of strengths and weaknesses.

It also gave a list of all players on every club's books, along with their height, weight, position, year signed for the club and where they had signed from.

'Dundee in big time' was the headline above the team pictured in last season's white change strip, before the guide declared Shankly's side was in 'fine fettle'.

It read, 'Same again? Why not? The mixture as before – or nearly so – should again be just as nasty-tasting medicine for opponents. European Cup? Well, all the best anyway!'

The European Cup draw had brought a renewed dose of football fever to Dundee, but that didn't stop the goalposts being pulled down and the markings washed away from the public pitches at Riverside Park.

Fledgling company Loganair had expressed interest in developing the site on the banks of the River Tay for flying to fill the gaps that the state airline would not or could not fill.

Loganair was established by flamboyant Scottish construction engineer Willie Logan, whose firm would go on to win the contract to build the Tay Road Bridge.

A small landing strip was eventually 'scraped out' across several of the old pitches about half a mile long in the grass to facilitate the ambitious proposal at Riverside.

A five-seater Piper Aztec touched down on the makeshift runway in August 1962, opposite the big top of Bertram Mills' Circus and Menagerie.

The travelling circus was in residence from the Olympia in West London although quite what the 'uncannily intelligent football elephants' thought of it all was anyone's guess.

The chartered flight received a welcome on the runway from Lord Provost Maurice McManus who said the city was now in the 'happy position' of knowing Riverside was suitable for chartered flights and spoke of the possibilities of opening up air links between Dundee and Aberdeen, Inverness, London, Gibraltar or Nice.

He said there was 'absolutely no reason' why Dundee FC supporters could not fly direct to Cologne to support their team in the European Cup in September.

Meanwhile, there was rebellion in the air with Alan Gilzean, Alex Hamilton, Andy Penman, Hugh Robertson, Bobby Seith and Ian Ure all wanting more than the £25 a week wages on offer. For his part, Shankly said that what they were being paid was a small fortune compared to his playing days with Falkirk, where he spent 13 years between 1933 and 1946.

He reminisced about his childhood growing up in the once-thriving coal mining community of Glenbuck in Ayrshire where the winters were cold and bitter.

The Shankly family – parents Barbara and John, along with their five sons (who all went on to become professional footballers) and five daughters – lived in a small cottage on Miners Row in the village.

Shankly told his players that his family was so poor that his mother used an old boiler for the weekly wash on Monday before making soup in it to last the rest of the week.

The impasse continued but just days before the start of the new campaign the deadlock was broken when Hamilton, Penman and Robertson re-signed.

The others did likewise soon afterwards.

Shankly declared himself to be 'glad it's all over, with everybody happy'.

Last to put pen to paper was Ure, who was fast establishing himself as one of the country's top defenders, having made his Scotland international breakthrough against Wales at Hampden in November 1961.

He said, 'It's been a worrying time for me.

'I'd like to make it clear that I'm happy with Dundee.

'There was no question of asking for a move. It was simply a matter of pounds, shillings and pence – and now I'm satisfied.'

All bar the out-of-favour Liney and the injured Seith were in the team for the opening game of the 1962/63 season, a League Cup sectional tie against city rivals Dundee United at Tannadice Park.

Dundee sported their new strip, described as 'a polo-neck jersey a la Real Madrid', but that was where the similarity ended as the city's lesser lights took the spoils.

Alan Gilzean twice gave Dundee the lead but the men in black and white pulled back twice with goals from Walter Carlyle before Jim Irvine grabbed a late winner.

The league flag was then raised by Lady Provost McManus to mark the club's first home game of the season, the second group game against Celtic.

It was raised on a specially erected flagpole behind the TC Keay traditional home end of the ground on 15 August 1962 in front of 20,000 fans.

Dundee defeated Celtic 1-0 with a Gordon Smith goal on 60 minutes but there were contrasting emotions for the team's two senior goalkeepers.

For Bert Slater, this was a new start, and with a stocky boxer's build and a nose that looked as if it had taken its fair share of punishment, his team-mates were quick to nickname him 'Punchy'.

It was a different story for championship hero Pat Liney, who had watched events from the main stand.

Somewhat surprisingly to many, Shankly had made it clear that Slater was his first-choice goalkeeper and Liney was now to find his appearances very limited indeed.

The Admiralty in London was also proving there was little room for sentiment when it came to tough decisions. The *Unicorn*, the oldest ship of the Royal Navy still afloat, was in the way of one of the approach roads for the new Tay Road Bridge.

Earl Grey Dock, where the 46-gun frigate was moored, was due to be filled in and it was decided the old lady should be broken up where she lay. The frigate was eventually given a reprieve after a deputation from Dundee went to London to argue the case and the Queen Mother joined calls to save the ship.

Agreement was reached that an attempt would be made to move her but if she started to break up during the tow she would be taken to deeper water and sunk.

The voyage that could save the *Unicorn* was scheduled to take place in October.

The city's Royal Arch, which gave access to one of the port's main docks, was also due to be wiped out because it too was in the way of the Tay Road Bridge landfall development.

On 23 August 1962, just a day after the *Unicorn*'s reprieve, Dundee's players and officials returned to the City Chambers where they had celebrated their title success on winning the league a few months earlier.

A civic reception was hosted by Lord Provost McManus to honour the league champions.

A cushion of blue and white flowers, emblazoned 'Dundee FC', greeted guests and the silver championship trophy was the centrepiece of the top table.

'Last season they accomplished the greatest feat of all,' said Mr McManus.

'They brought the league championship to the city for the first time.

'I am sure that all the citizens, particularly the football fans, the directors of the club, the manager and the trainer must have been very proud of the lads last year.

'It is a tremendous task to win a championship but experience has shown that while it may be difficult to win a championship it's doubly difficult to retain it.

'You can rest assured every football fan in the city will be keen to see you make a success of your run in the European Cup.'

'We have no delusions, no ideas, that we are on an easy thing,' said Dundee chairman James Gellatly.

'But I can assure you the boys will do their best.'

Mr Gellatly told the Lord Provost that Dundee's success was the culmination of much effort over a long period of years.

He paid tribute to the late George Anderson, who had laid down the short passing system during his ten years as manager between 1944 and 1954.

Anderson was the man who guided Dundee to their first major trophies in over 40 years with back-to-back League Cup successes in the early 1950s.

As well as those League Cups, the flamboyant Anderson was best remembered as the man who signed 'pocket dynamo' Billy Steel for a Scottish record fee in 1950.

Mr Gellatly then called each player, manager Bob Shankly and trainer Sammy Kean to receive their league medals at the civic reception.

All was not well in the camp, however, for with just one win from the four games played so far, there were considerable tensions behind the scenes.

Things came to a head when Andy Penman, stung by criticism from his team-mates for not pulling his weight during a training match, handed in a transfer request.

Child protégé Penman joined Everton straight from school in Dunfermline and made his debut aged 15 before he got homesick and signed for Dundee in 1959.

Dundee's youngest-ever player, known as the 'Penalty King' for his precision from the spot, said, 'I am sure I would benefit by leaving Dens Park and I would not mind going to England.

'I'll just have to wait and see what happens.

'I am determined to leave anyway.'

The City Square would become the scene of similar protest the following week when Dr Richard Beeching stopped off on his way to Aberdeen on 27 August.

Beeching left the diesel train during a scheduled three-minute halt at Tay Bridge Station and chatted on the platform with stationmaster Richard Turner.

Beeching was wielding his axe over the British rail network with plans to cut over 5,000 miles of track and more than 2,000 stations.

Rail workers in Dundee stopped work and took part in a protest against the cuts when they marched to the City Square with placards and called for a national strike.

* * *

The protest against the cuts provoked further disruption when the Dundee squad arrived in Glasgow for a midweek game when Dr Beeching was also making an official visit.

Rail workshop employees stopped work for two hours across Scotland during the talks at the Scottish Region of British Railways in Glasgow on 29 August.

The 4,500 Glasgow demonstrators were joined by four 'pall bearers' who carried a coffin with the simple message 'BR – Scottish Region' planted on the side.

Dundee's poor showing in a 3-0 League Cup defeat to Celtic later that evening contributed towards them finishing bottom of their group with only four points.

Wolves manager Stan Cullis watched the match to check on several players including Alex Hamilton, Ian Ure and Alan Gilzean.

Cullis wanted to strengthen his squad but Dundee were not prepared to sell any first-team player until after the European Cup tie against Cologne.

By the time the first leg came round on 5 September things had worsened.

Dundee had now lost to Dundee United, Celtic and Hearts (twice) in the League Cup, and their only league outing had ended in another defeat to Hearts.

Dr Beeching was preparing to take a hefty sledgehammer to Britain's railways just as Dundee's season was already in danger of running out of steam.

The European Cup was to provide the perfect platform to get things back on track.

Chapter 2

Smoke and Mirrors

*'It's far better to meet a British club in
September than in November or December
when the grounds are heavy.'*

Cologne goalkeeper Fritz Ewert

EXPECTATIONS WERE so low that just ten fans
put their names forward for a special flight to mark the
club's first venture into the unknown.

The Dundee Supporters' Club had tried to organise
a direct 36-seater charter flight from Edinburgh to
Cologne for the second leg on 26 September. But
Dundee had lost five of their first seven games of the
season and it was clear that many fans weren't giving
their team much of a chance of still being in the tie
after the first leg.

The charter flight was off – for now.

The *Sporting Post* put forward a similar proposal which was gathering more interest by offering ten all-expenses-paid trips to Cologne including a match ticket. The entry form asked Dundee fans to pick a team from a selection of 33 past and present players at their peak. A judging panel was then set up to give ten prizes to 'the most meritorious entries'.

Cologne were among the favourites to win the competition and boasted no fewer than ten West German internationals including 1954 World Cup winner Hans Schäfer. Regarded as one of his country's greatest wingers, Schäfer also captained West Germany to the semi-finals and quarter-finals of the 1958 and 1962 World Cups.

Karl-Heinz Schnellinger, who was named in the best team of the 1962 competition, was considered to be one of the best and most complete left-backs in the world. Schnellinger was also named West German Footballer of the Year ahead of the legendary Uwe Seeler for his performances during Cologne's title-winning season.

Striker Karl-Heinz Thielen had finished top scorer for Cologne with 24 goals in 29 games and combined his playing career with studying business and economics.

The West German champions were due to arrive in Scotland two days before the match. There was huge interest in the first leg with tickets priced from five shillings to £1. They would not lack support when they finally arrived in Dundee with over 100 fans flying in on chartered flights put on by two Cologne newspapers.

Cologne assistant secretary Karl Fröhlich was already in the city and had watched the Dark Blues go down 3-0 to Celtic and 2-0 to Hearts in the League Cup. Fröhlich was on a scouting mission while also finalising arrangements for the use of training facilities for when Cologne arrived.

He spent the Sunday after the Hearts game at Tynecastle on the golf course at Monifieth where he was carrying the bags for some new friends he made in Dundee.

'I played one shot and decided to give up golf,' he said. 'In Cologne there is only one golf club with about a hundred members catering for a population of one million. I found strolling around the links much more relaxing than watching football and what's more, I found four balls.

'I was a bit disappointed with your champions but Ure, was, for me, the best player on the field. I did tell him when I was in his company that he does one thing wrong. He plays far too much football for a player with a number five on his jersey.

'I think we should have an excellent game and I may say we are glad to be playing a team like Dundee, for, with our style, we don't like rough teams.'

West Germany and the European Cup already had a grim link to Dundee following the death of journalist Charlie Caw, who covered matches for *The People*.

Caw was born in Dundee in 1894 and should have been a passenger on the plane which killed Manchester United's Busby Babes in 1958. United were travelling from Yugoslavia following a 3-3 draw with Red Star Belgrade in the European Cup quarter-final when the plane stopped in Munich to refuel. Mystery still surrounds why Caw never took his seat on the European Airways Flight 609 which crashed at Munich-Riem Airport in West Germany. A late change of plan meant that somebody took his place and that he changed planes.

But, in a cruel twist of fate, two days after the air disaster he died of a heart attack and hypertension.

It was a sliding doors moment, but with a sad ending.

The West German champions, who played at the 65,000-capacity Müngersdorfer Stadium, travelled to Scotland in confident mood following a 2-1 derby win over Viktoria Cologne watched by 20,000 fans. The low turnout was put down to glorious weather in Cologne which prompted Germans to scramble for the sun-loungers instead of the terraces.

Herr Fröhlich was celebrating his birthday when the German party of 39 left Cologne for Edinburgh on a KLM aircraft on Monday, 3 September at 11am. Midfielder Hans Sturm was also celebrating his 27th birthday, although he was struggling after picking up an ankle injury in the derby game.

Sturm played in the 1958 and 1962 World Cups for West Germany and he kept his injured foot high in the air during the plane journey to Edinburgh. The air crew on the charter flight managed to lift his spirits when he received a birthday gift from the airline of a manicure set.

Sturm was also given extra recovery time before the Dundee game when the arrival of the plane was delayed for 40 minutes by thick fog in Edinburgh. The squad boarded buses on arrival that took them straight to the

Royal British Hotel in Castle Street, which was chosen for Cologne's base in Dundee.

Cologne arrived at 5.40pm in torrential rain and goalkeeper Fritz Ewert said he was confident they could weather the storm and could go all the way in the competition.

'It's far better to meet a British club in September than in November or December when the grounds are heavy,' he said. 'British teams are more at home in these conditions.'

One player who was missing from the Cologne party was midfielder Ernst-Günter Habig, who played for West Germany at the 1956 Melbourne Olympics. Habig was terrified of flying and was making the 24-hour trip by car, rail and sea.

The manager of the restaurant at the Müngersdorfer Stadium was being sent along as his travelling companion, although there was no room for the team mascot.

In 1950, a local circus gave the newly formed Cologne a young billy goat as a present for good luck and he took the name of manager Hennes Weisweiler. Cologne adopted Hennes as their mascot and he became a fixture at home matches, and even travelled to away games on the team bus! On this occasion Cologne's goat mascot remained behind in West Germany with a regal stable to himself and freshly laid grass to graze on.

Cologne's manager was Zlatko Čajkovski who was regarded as one of the best Yugoslavian players ever, winning 55 caps for his country and scoring seven goals. He was a defensive midfielder and played for Yugoslavia at the Olympics in 1948 and 1952, winning the silver medal on both occasions. He also participated in the World Cups of 1950 and 1954 and joined Cologne in 1955 from Partizan Belgrade where he spent nine years and played almost 400 games.

Čajkovski gained his coaching badges at the German Sports Academy in Cologne under Weisweiler before finishing his playing career in Israel. He returned to Cologne in the summer of 1961 to take the top job and made history as the manager of the team which brought the club its first championship.

Čajkovski told the media in broken English that he could remember playing against Dundee winger Smith when Scotland played Yugoslavia in Belgrade in 1955. Smith scored the equaliser in the friendly game which finished 2-2 and was one of 18 games he played for Scotland between 1946 and 1957. The 39-year-old

Čajkovski then predicted Smith would end up on the losing side at Dens Park.

Čajkovski said he was putting a strategy in place based on a scouting report from Fröhlich, who had watched Dundee lose twice. He said, 'These plans are flexible and will be changed if the occasion demands. We will not be playing a defensive game. We won the championship by playing an aggressive, intelligent game – why change it now even if we could?'

Cologne's attacking philosophy was good news for Dundee, who had struggled to break down counter-attacking West German sides Reutlingen and Saarbrücken while in the USA.

'I have heard good and bad reports about Dundee,' said Čajkovski. 'I don't anticipate an easy match.'

Čajkovski was known as the 'complete boss', but he denied he was a hard taskmaster.

'All the players are my friends,' he said. 'They know what is expected of them. And I don't mind if they have an occasional glass of beer.'

Dundee spent that Monday training indoors because of the heavy rain in the city.

Shankly went through his tactics for the first leg in the afternoon before Ian Ure retired to the walls of the

Dens Park pavilion to work on his touch. Ure put in extra practice every afternoon and would go through his famed keepie-uppie routine for 45 minutes, managing as many as 6,000 touches without the ball hitting the ground. The Scotland international was also thumping shots against the wooden-sparred walls inside the main door with his weaker foot and showed great skill in collecting all the rebounds.

Fröhlich had organised a training session for Cologne at Dens later that evening to allow the West German players to get used to the floodlights and the match ball. Cologne's ball exercises were expected to be restricted to a spot behind the goal because the rain had left the Dens pitch soaked from the relentless downpour.

There was already great activity at the ground despite the weather with telephone engineers installing new lines for the use of the West German media. Television engineers were also busy as the game was to be shown live on the Eurovision link.

Shankly and trainer Sammy Kean remained at the ground to welcome the Cologne party but were kept waiting after Čajkovski cancelled training as a result of the weather.

Shankly and Kean didn't hang around. They left Dens and decided to call in on the team at the Royal British Hotel but were still one step behind when they got to the reception desk. The entire party had gone for a short walk around the city centre after an early meal.

The Cologne team walkabout passed the La Scala cinema in Murraygate where the West German party were confronted by the ghosts of the past.

The cinema was showing the documentary *Murder by Signature*, originally titled *Eichmann and the Third Reich*. The timing of the feature might have been slightly ill-judged with Anglo-German relations still delicate just 17 years from the end of the Second World War.

More appealing viewing was *Five Finger Exercise* at the Playhouse in Nethergate, *All Fall Down* at the ABC in Seagate or *The Pirates of Blood River* at the Plaza in the Hilltown. The Cologne players returned to the hotel following the short walk for a brisk rub-down from Hungarian masseur Josef Bocsai before retiring to bed.

Around 140 Cologne supporters flew in to Scotland the following day. The plucky Manfred Steinwarz was among the party arriving on Tuesday after sending a begging letter to Lord Provost McManus before the match.

'As I am an enthusiastic supporter of Cologne FC I would like to visit your city during my leave to see the game between Dundee FC and Cologne FC,' he said. 'All my attempts to get a ticket for the game have been in vain and I am writing to ask if it is possible for you to get a ticket for me. I hope you will not leave this German supporter in the lurch. Hoping to visit your splendid city soon.'

The direct approach – and no doubt the chance for the Lord Provost to generate some positive publicity in the local newspapers – had the desired effect. Mr McManus purchased a ticket and it was sent on to Herr Steinwarz.

Norbert Prinz, a 23-year-old amateur footballer from Saarbrücken, was another West German who arrived in Dundee for free. He won a sports quiz competition in the *Kicker* newspaper, which was confidently giving free travel to all Cologne's European Cup ties 'right up to the final'.

Ernst-Günter Habig was welcomed to the city by his team-mates when he arrived by car following his

24-hour journey from Cologne. Habig dropped off his bags at the team hotel before joining the squad for a 30-minute training session at junior team Dundee Violet's Glenesk Park.

The switch to a junior ground was because the Dens Park pitch was now being saved for Wednesday night after being battered by heavy rain. The Cologne players arrived at Dens in a fleet of taxis, had a quick look at the pitch, collected half a dozen balls and carried on to Violet's ground.

Shankly decided to organise a game between his own first team and the reserves at East End Park, Stobswell's junior ground, on the opposite side of the city. The Dundee party met their opponents before they went their separate ways and they exchanged pleasantries with each other despite the language barrier.

At Glenesk Park, the Cologne players were split up into little groups by Čajkovski and took part in short passing exercises for the first 15 minutes of the session. Čajkovski then called them all together and they walked, jogged, then ran up the park, doing various exercises to relax the muscles.

Cologne were apparently under a cloud following their own slow start to the season, but it didn't seem to affect team spirit considering the high-jinks during the loosening-up exercises. The Cologne players were on a £45 bonus if they beat Dundee.

The West Germans had already announced their team apart from the left-half position, but it was now starting to look like they would be faced with fresh injury worries.

Hans Sturm, who was nursing an injured ankle following the derby win, was still being given treatment and didn't take any part in the training session. Right-back Georg Stollenwerk did take part but was complaining of a stiff neck following the brief workout. Stollenwerk earned 23 international caps between 1951 and 1960 and took part in the 1952 Helsinki Olympics and the 1958 World Cup in Sweden. Stollenwerk said he could hardly move his neck.

Dr James Simpson, Dundee's medical advisor, was called out. He examined the 31-year-old defender and diagnosed the pain as coming from a strained shoulder muscle but thought he would be fit in time for the match. Stollenwerk was advised to rest up following the training session, but he was later taken to hospital to be given an injection to dull the pain. Things started to go from bad to worse for Cologne.

Striker Christian Müller limped off the park and World Cup winner Hans Schäfer joined him on the sidelines after complaining about a pain in his leg. The injuries were stacking up, but only Hans Sturm was expected to miss the first leg.

Čajkovski wasn't taking any chances though. He sent out an urgent SOS to Cologne, where reserve forward Wolfgang Tripp was told to drop everything and fly over to Scotland.

Meanwhile, Ian Ure was the target for German camera crews after Dundee's own training session when he performed some ball tricks on the pavement outside the ground. Ure's party piece impressed, but the German writers were underwhelmed by what they witnessed at the Stobswell practice match, where Dundee tried out a new style.

Kicker journalist Robert Becker said British football was highly regarded in West Germany but warned that Cologne were an attacking side who were not afraid of Dundee.

At this point Shankly decided to go back to basics and scrapped plans to change his formation following the poor showing under the watchful eye of the media. For days Shankly and Kean had drilled the Dundee players in training and tactical talks on exactly how they were to play against Cologne.

The Shankly plan was developed following the poor start to the season because his team were shipping goals far too easily while not scoring themselves. Shankly knew that Cologne's main attacking threat came from the wings.

He decided to change the way his side would play, but he stopped the game four times with the reserves a goal ahead because the first team couldn't grasp the new set-up. Eventually he called another halt to proceedings.

'Okay, you are obviously not fully happy about the change,' he told his players. 'Let's play our usual game and see what happens.'

Right away the first team clicked and scored a couple of quick goals. Shankly decided to scrap any plans to be more defensively minded in the first leg.

'I could see they didn't quite get the hang of what I wanted them to do,' he said. 'They were thinking too much on what they had to do, rather than doing it. As soon as I told them to revert to their normal game, for the first time this season they showed flashes of their old form.'

Cologne manager Čajkovski sought out the four German journalists when they returned from watching Dundee's training session at Stobswell. 'Do Dundee play 4-2-4?' he asked.

Dundee journalists believed Čajkovski's line of questioning gave weight to the fact that Cologne might have been running a bluff in their air of confidence.

The rain would return with a vengeance on Tuesday afternoon when a one-hour cloudburst brought some of the worst flooding to hit the city in many years.

The fire brigade had over 20 call-outs within an hour requesting pumping assistance at flooded premises and basements. The city's Wellgate steps became a waterfall, due to the floods running down the Hilltown.

The Cologne players climbed to the top of Dundee Law that evening, providing the perfect viewing platform to see panoramic views of the city and the River Tay. They were joined by Wolfgang Tripp, who had flown in from West Germany on standby following the injury concerns to key players.

Tripp, who topped his amateur league scoring chart the previous season with 40 goals for Marburg, arrived ahead of schedule at 9.30pm. His plane was actually late but he caught another train north, changing at Edinburgh. The 19-year-old schoolboy might have earned top marks for punctuality but he was now told he was unlikely to be needed after all.

The news from the camp was that Stollenwerk and Schnellinger would miss the first leg with injury but Hans Sturm was expected to be fit.

On Wednesday morning, Cologne's support was further enhanced by 41 West German soldiers from the 8th Panzer Division who arrived in Carnoustie. The soldiers – one officer, six sergeants and 34 men – were all passionate supporters of Cologne and had been training at the tank ranges at Castlemartin in Wales. They decided to travel to Dundee to watch the first leg and were being put up for the night at the Barry Buddon camp by the 1st Battalion of the Black Watch.

The soldiers admitted they wouldn't see much of the city during their stay as they planned to return to Wales the following morning. The West Germans unfurled a banner on arrival which said: 'The boys from Cologne send greetings to the Scots boys.' There was harmony in the air – for now.

Elsewhere, a tea-swilling chimp was being given the red carpet treatment in Dundee alongside the West German champions. Rosie, the star of the PG Tips TV adverts, arrived to open a Fine Fare supermarket in Ardler just before the first leg, with parents urged to 'bring the children along to see her antics'. Rosie was given a guard of honour by the band of the Dagenham Girl Pipers before she opened the supermarket.

Such pleasantries were in short supply at Dens Park, where Cologne were being accused of trying to pull a fast one over their injury worries. 'They are a first-class side and we are paying no attention to all the talk about their injured list and team doubts,' said Bob Shankly.

Čajkovski did not schedule any training before the match. The Cologne players were told to go to bed in the afternoon to rest up and the team was scheduled to arrive at Dens an hour before kick-off.

Fröhlich joined the smoke-and-mirrors ploy before the match when he suggested the team selection could still be changed at the eleventh hour.

He said, 'We may switch about our attack but we will make that decision when we have tested the ground conditions. It will probably be a little heavy after all that rain. We have never seen it rain as it did in your city yesterday afternoon.'

The Dundee team reported to Dens before kick-off and Shankly praised the effort his players had been putting in on the training field to reverse their fortunes.

'We have never worked so hard before to try to win any game,' said Shankly. 'A win is doubly important. Apart from advancing our chances for the second game in Cologne it could put us back on the rails. All our boys need is a little confidence and a win over Cologne tonight will bring it back.'

Now was the time for heroes.

Chapter 3

The Blitzkrieg that left the German Embassy Reeling

'I've never seen them play this way before.'

Cologne assistant secretary Karl Fröhlich

DESPITE THE difficult start to the season, Shankly was taking heart from the fact that his misfiring side always seemed to step up and play better on the big occasion.

Various permutations had been tried with reserves Bobby Waddell, Alex Stuart, Craig Brown, Doug Houston and Kenny Cameron brought in without success. That's why – with the exception of goalkeeper Pat Liney – he decided to name the same team that won the First Division title.

The *Evening Telegraph* produced a souvenir programme in colour to mark the occasion. The supplement included a message from chairman James Gellatly, who said Shankly's desire to play attractive football was the reason for Dundee's success.

'We are very pleased that by winning the league we qualified to participate in the European Cup for the first time and are so granted the opportunity of bringing one of the top continental sides to Dundee,' he said. 'We are happy to welcome Cologne to our city this evening. They come with a very high reputation for the quality of their football and determination and we realise this match is certainly a tough assignment for us.'

The date was Wednesday, 5 September 1962.

Dundee's first flirtation with Europe was predicted to last no longer than the preliminary round and Cologne were the overwhelming favourites to progress.

Although the Dark Blues were untested at this level, winger Gordon Smith could take confidence that he was no stranger to putting West German opposition to the sword. Smith was part of the legendary Hibs 'Famous Five' team which defeated Bayern Munich 6-1 during a tour of Germany, Austria and Switzerland in 1950.

Thousands of cars began arriving at Dens Park from 6pm onwards and quickly the streets in the immediate vicinity of the ground were full. The congestion wasn't being helped by the fact that part of Gussie Park was still being used for a carnival and all the space available was soon taken up by cars and buses.

An hour before kick-off, a double rainbow lit up the wild sky from the city centre and one end seemed to land at Dens Park, which would prove to be a lucky omen.

Inside the dressing room most of the Dundee players were quietly confident. Not one of them appeared to have paid the slightest bit of attention to the big talk and pre-match bluster which had been coming out of the West German camp.

The biggest man on the pitch at Dens was referee Carl Frederick Jørgensen of Denmark, who was six foot three inches tall. He was a referee at the 1952 Olympics and 1958 World Cup.

Jørgensen, who was in the textile trade, and his Danish linesmen Aage Poulsen and Einar Poulsen, were driven to Dens following a conducted tour of Keiller's sweet factory. The sugary treat had been arranged by another local official, John Gordon, who was a referee who worked in the cashier's department at the Maryfield plant.

Legendary commentator Kenneth Wolstenholme was high up in the gantry for the first-leg match to call proceedings for the BBC radio and television coverage.

Highlights of the match would be shown on *Sports Special for Scotland* at 10.45pm, followed by coverage of Rangers' game against Seville in the European Cup Winners' Cup, taking place on the same evening.

Wolstenholme was the voice of football on the BBC. He was no stranger to heights, and no stranger to the Germans. His journalism career was put on hold during the Second World War while he trained as an RAF bomber pilot before flying 100 missions over Germany.

That was a hazardous existence indeed and Wolstenholme was awarded the Distinguished Flying Cross and Bar, the 1939–1945 Star, Air Crew Europe Star with France and Germany Bar, Defence Medal and War Medal.

Wolstenholme had just returned from spending the summer in Chile where he covered 18 matches at the 1962 World Cup with David Coleman and two camera crews. The Battle of Santiago – a violent encounter between Chile and Italy – was nothing compared to the pounding the Dens Park pitch had taken from the torrential rain. But the ground staff had made sure it was in perfect condition ahead of kick-off.

It was more than could be said for Dundee's training gear. The players warmed up on the pitch for their maiden voyage into Europe in ripped tracksuit bottoms. The West German heroes, in contrast, were resplendent in new tracksuits and they were looking every inch the superstar outfit.

Anticipation and excitement was at fever pitch as the fans began moving through the Dens Park turnstiles for Dundee's first European game under the lights.

As the thousands of supporters came through the gates and found themselves a spot on the terracing, the tremendous atmosphere was enhanced by the high walls of the Bowbridge jute works off Dens Road.

The reflection from the floodlights illuminated the dark Dundee sky as the champions of Scotland and West Germany were piped on by the instrumental band of the Black Watch. The pipe band played the Dundee anthem 'Up Wi' The Bonnets' and performed the national anthems of both countries before kick-off.

The European Cup was widely acknowledged as the biggest money spinner in world football, although a top continental club visiting Dens wasn't a new thing. Dundee had played against European opposition in the Anglo-Franco-Scottish Friendship Cup where they defeated Valenciennes of France 4-3 on aggregate. Scotland won the inaugural edition of the short-lived tournament in 1960, which also included Celtic, Clyde, Motherwell, Lens, Sedan and Toulouse.

There was also a friendly match against Swedish champions Elfsborg in November 1961 where Andy Penman scored five goals in an 8-2 win.

The big question among the 25,000 crowd was whether Dundee could put their poor domestic form to one side and rise to the occasion when it mattered most.

Dundee: Slater, Hamilton, Cox, Seith, Ure, Wishart, Smith, Penman, Cousin, Gilzean, Robertson.

Cologne: Ewert, Regh, Sturm, Hemmersbach, Wilden, Benthaus, Thielen, Schäfer, Müller, Habig, Hornig.

The Dundee players decided to revert to the V-neck jerseys they had worn during the title-winning season rather than the new continental-style crew-neck outfit. Maybe it helped Dundee to turn back the clock to the season before since they blew Cologne out of the water with perhaps the greatest performance in the club's history.

They went on the attack straight from the start.

Goalkeeper Fritz Ewert was forced to save with his legs from Alan Gilzean after clever combination work from Hugh Robertson and Alan Cousin. Ewert was then hurt in the second minute when he went up for a high ball with Cousin, although nobody realised it would have serious consequences for Cologne.

The goalkeeper staggered back to his goal before he collapsed. He was laid out cold on the pitch before getting back to his feet after receiving treatment. Ewert resumed to face the Dundee barrage despite suffering from concussion.

The home side scored three goals in three minutes. The first came on ten minutes when Seith put Penman through with a defence-splitting pass. Penman then fired in a low cross from the right which was headed into his own net by Matthias Hemmersbach.

Two minutes later Hugh Robertson found Bobby Wishart on the edge of the box. Wishart made it two with a strike which Dundee reserve Craig Brown later described as 'the most incredible goal I have ever seen'.

The Dundee left-half took a swing but kicked the ground before the ball. The ball trundled one way and a huge divot went in the opposite direction.

Ewert dived across his goal to save the divot. The ball rolled gently past him into the corner of the net.

The crowd struggled to comprehend what they had just witnessed and Kenneth Wolstenholme even paused for breath during his BBC commentary!

Dundee went three-up 60 seconds later. Alex Hamilton sent over a cross to the far post. Robertson got on the end of it and his shot was deflected past Ewert off the unlucky Anton Regh to complete three goals in three minutes.

Dens Park was in a frenzy and the Dundee fans danced on the terracing. Some spilled out on to the track to celebrate the quick goals.

Cologne fought back and Christian Müller brought out two great saves from Bert Slater. But this was Dundee's night and back they came.

Alan Gilzean went close when he struck the bar with a fierce drive. Then Dundee went 4-0 up on 26 minutes.

Ian Ure started the move when he brought the ball out from the back before supplying Gilzean, whose cross-field pass found Smith on the right wing. Smith crossed for Gilzean to head home and Dens erupted once again.

Cologne still looked dangerous on the break but were struggling to get past Cox and Ure.

On 38 minutes Dundee did everything but score. Penman struck the post and Bobby Seith missed by inches with a shot.

Dundee made it 5-0 just before half-time thanks to Gordon Smith, who was described in the souvenir programme as 'the greatest soccer pin up north of the border since the war'.

Gilzean had burst through but his shot was saved by Ewert. Smith stayed cool under pressure and scored from the rebound.

Dundee were a team transformed and all the fight and hunger that thus far had been lacking this season was back. The team left the field at half-time to a tremendous ovation from their fans.

It's said windows on Provost Road and Sandeman Street shook and shuddered from a level of decibels never heard before, or since.

The West German champions came out for the second half without their goalkeeper Ewert, who failed to recover from his accidental collision with Cousin. He had two stitches inserted in a cut over his mouth but was clearly still dazed. Ewert thought the score was only 2-0 when he went in at the break and didn't believe it when his team-mates told him he had lost another three goals.

Anton Regh was forced to pull on his jumper and take his place between the sticks. With no substitutes in those days, Cologne were now down to ten men.

The one-man advantage looked likely to kill off whatever slight chance they had of staging a miraculous comeback.

Dundee showed no mercy.

They simply picked up where they left off. Cologne were outclassed in every department.

The Dark Blues were moving the ball fast and with deadly accuracy. Captain Bobby Cox, who later bought the Lorne Bar in Broughty Ferry and renamed it The Sliding Tackle, was leading by example from the back.

Dundee got number six when Gilzean sent Robertson away down the left. The winger cut inside and crossed for Penman to score with a header from close range.

Cologne kept fighting despite being 6-0 down. Thielen struck the bar and then had another shot brilliantly saved by Slater. But Dundee looked like scoring every time they went up the pitch.

Gilzean made it seven on 64 minutes with a bullet header from Hamilton's cross. He went on to complete his hat-trick three minutes later. It was another header – this time from a cross by his strike partner Cousin.

A deflection off full-back Hamilton from a cross by Ernst-Günter Habig gave Cologne a consolation on 71 minutes. The West Germans gained momentum from the goal and captain Hans Schäfer almost pulled a second back when he hit the bar with a 25-yard effort.

With 12 minutes left and rain starting to fall once again, Cologne team coach Čajkovski was ordered away from behind the goal by the referee. He was guilty of coaching his replacement goalkeeper Regh.

Just on full time, Penman almost made it nine when his shot was saved by Regh from close range after he snaked past three defenders.

Regh conceded just three goals after taking over from Ewert but he stressed after the match that he 'could do nothing' to stop any of them.

Hundreds of Dundee fans surged on to the field at full time to congratulate their heroes.

Dundee had 23 shots on goal, with their ten-man opponents only able to muster six.

The Dark Blues sportingly lined up at full time to clap the Cologne team up the tunnel. Fans were singing as they walked down Dens Road, which was packed wall-to-wall. They were in great spirits despite getting a soaking from the heavy rain.

Wolstenholme was also singing Dundee's praises from the gantry. He told BBC listeners that he rated the Dark Blues as one of the best sides he had ever seen and predicted they could go all the way in the competition.

The 8-1 victory made headlines throughout Europe, though it was probably best summarised by former Dundee player and local football writing legend Tommy Gallacher. He was the son of the peerless Patsy – the legendary Celtic player from the 1920s – but he became a stalwart in his own right for Dundee before a second career opened up after he hung up his boots in 1956.

The Courier journalist described the display as 'a magnificent brand of cultured precision football that far outshone any of their performances in bringing home the league title'.

'German champions smothered in 8-goal avalanche' was the headline. Gallacher said the 'crowd were cheering like they'd never cheered before at Dens'.

Shankly was just as fulsome in his praise for his team when he spoke to the media. He said, 'I am delighted. My boys rose to the occasion as I expected them to. Naturally it puts us in a very strong position for the return but we will not be letting up.'

Dundee's victory tally was two more than they had scored in all their opening seven games and their highest tally since that 8-2 win against Elfsborg.

Cologne captain Schäfer said, 'We were surprised because we thought this was a defensive team we were meeting.'

The official attendance was 24,500, with gate receipts generated for Dundee in the region of £8,500.

Children who were playing late near the ground in Sandeman Street also struck gold when Cologne supporters emptied their pockets of loose change before their journey home.

Dens was not the only place where there was a shock result in Europe. Part-time Bangor City from the Cheshire League defeated star-studded Italian side Napoli 2-0 at home in the European Cup Winners' Cup.

All in all, it was a great night for British teams. Rangers also won 4-0 against Seville at Ibrox in the Cup Winners' Cup. Only Linfield from Northern Ireland failed to make it a clean sweep when they went down 2-1 at home to Danish side Esbjerg in the European Cup.

Real Madrid, the five-time winners of the competition, were also in danger of joining Cologne on the first-round scrapheap. They were booed off at the Bernabeu by their own fans after being held to a 3-3 draw by the Belgian champions Anderlecht despite twice being in front.

Were we witnessing a changing of the guard in European football?

Cologne proved they were still box office despite the 8-1 drubbing. A crowd of 100 people gathered outside the Royal British Hotel to watch the disappointed team arriving back after the game. There was then the traditional banquet, where the players and officials of Dundee and Cologne ate a hearty but late meal together.

The evening went on longer than expected due to the difficulties of interpreting the speeches. That was down to the fact that Karl Fröhlich, the best English speaker in the Cologne party, wasn't in attendance.

Fröhlich snubbed the bash and instead sat in the TV lounge in the hotel in shirt sleeves and socks bemoaning his team's disappointing display. He was the most disillusioned member of the party in Dundee that night.

'I've never seen them play this way before,' he said. 'It was contrary to the close-marking plan they were supposed to work to. Smith and Penman had far too much room. All the discussions and conferences went for nothing.

'Our players are not hungry enough. The club provide them with businesses and professions and on this showing football becomes a sideline. Dundee are true professionals.'

Cologne were also seething over Cousin's early challenge which had left goalkeeper Ewert concussed after just two minutes of the match.

Cousin, of course, saw it differently when he addressed the media. He said, 'It really was a completely accidental collision, the type that happens in most games. Although losing their keeper was clearly a blow, we produced a wonderful performance at home.'

Cousin was the last player anyone would believe capable of deliberately hurting an opponent and he put the 8-1 win down to the experience in the Dundee side.

He singled out people like Bobby Wishart, a title-winner with Aberdeen, Bobby Seith, who won the league in England, and Gordon Smith, who won titles with Hibs and Hearts. He also hailed the team spirit which he said 'really helped when we were up against it'.

Fröhlich hadn't seen any of the second half because he stayed behind in the dressing room with Ewert when the goalkeeper was unable to continue at the break.

He also had no idea who scored his side's consolation goal but stayed up to watch the TV highlights before he quietly departed in his stockinged feet.

Bobby Seith, who lived in Barnhill, got the green-and-cream liveried number 10 bus home after the dinner with Bobby Wishart, who lived in Aberdeen but was staying overnight with Seith. It would have been hard to imagine Real Madrid stars Ferenc Puskas or Alfredo di Stefano getting a local bus home after a European game!

The misfiring Cologne team left their Dundee hotel downbeat at 7.30 the following morning to board the bus which would take them to the airport.

Dundee took it easy with some light practice following what was being described in some quarters as the team's greatest moment since the war. Alan Gilzean said, 'It did our morale a power of good. We felt we could hold our own now with any club and that was far from how we felt before Cologne came to Dens Park.'

Alex Hamilton was receiving treatment for two boils on his thigh but it was nothing compared to the pain being felt by Cologne. A spokesman from the German Embassy in London was still struggling to take in the Dundee blitzkrieg.

'I can't understand it,' he said. 'It is inexplicable, beyond comprehension. It will bring a sense of shame to all German sports supporters. Our players cannot claim that they lack international experience but our defence was left so hopeless. All credit must go to the Dundee forward line.'

He said he had been surprised at the directness of Dundee's football.

Cologne flew back home to West Germany in disgrace from Edinburgh at midday although Karl

Fröhlich predicted his team would at least win the return match.

'Dundee will be beaten in Cologne on September 26,' he said. 'We played very badly and the slippery ground does not help our style of play. If we have it dry as we like it I am sure we will win next time – although I have no hopes at all that we can get near Dundee on aggregate.'

Alf Ramsey, whose Ipswich side had pipped Burnley and Tottenham Hotspur by a handful of points, were England's representatives.

Ramsey, the former Spurs defender, who went on to guide England to World Cup glory in 1966, was fulsome in his praise for Dundee in the run-up to his own team's first game of the competition against Floriana of Malta.

He said, 'I saw Cologne last season and would have rated them one of the strongest teams in the competition. Dundee's performance was terrific.'

Bob Miller's popular *People's Journal* column also hailed Dundee's return to form following their trials and tribulations on the domestic front. He said, 'Here we had the old, hard-hitting Dark Blues on the form that downed Rangers last season and brought them the league championship. We had 11 men dedicated to their job. They went out resolute in purpose and they did their job in first-class fashion.

'I know Dundee go to Cologne on September 26 for the return game. They'll get it rough and tough, but I fancy they'll hold their own. It can be taken as written that they're in the next round and the fans will be looking for another first-class attraction at Dens Park. I'll bet, too, that more that 25,000 will turn out to see the game.'

Football was later put into perspective when news broke of the death of a Dundee legend. Jimmy Lawson, who signed from Carnoustie Panmure in 1905, passed away suddenly in the Bahamas where he was working in the world of golf.

Lawson became the regular right-back and helped the team win the 1910 Scottish Cup, Dundee's first major trophy, following victory against Clyde. While playing for Dundee, Lawson also gained recognition when he represented the Scottish League against the Irish League. Just before the First World War he left for America where he helped Bethlehem Steel Works win the American Cup.

Lawson became one of the few men to gain both Scottish and American cup medals. A first-class golfer who had won the first two Scottish Footballers' Golf Championships, he took up the sport professionally after hanging up his boots. Lawson was then a golf professional in America before retiring to live in Florida.

In 1958 he agreed to do some work at the ultra-exclusive Lyford Cay Club in Nassau, where he won the friendship of hundreds of business tycoons, millionaires and titled visitors. Lawson's remains were shipped back to Dunedin, Florida, where he lived with his wife.

Back in Dundee, tobacco prohibitionists were defeated at the City Chambers the day after Cologne's European Cup hopes had gone up in smoke. In three separate debates it was decided not to ban smoking in public places despite new cases of lung cancer in the city having increased by 50% in the past year.

The German newspapers recognised Dundee were the far better side and didn't give Cologne the slightest chance of turning the tie around in the return leg.

The Frankfurt evening paper *Abendpost* said Cologne were beaten by 'the brilliant trumps of the Scots' and said that 'the German team was knocked completely out of its stride by Dundee's bewildering play'.

However, an unforgiving element of the West German media were looking for a scapegoat and some of them used a freak photo to prove there was no smoke without fire.

They blamed the early injury to the goalkeeper as the main reason for the heavy defeat and published a picture in which Cousin appeared to punch Ewert in the face.

It was a photograph which was to provide the main fuel for a return leg which would become known as the Battle of Cologne.

Chapter 4

Planes, Trains and Automobiles

'Well, we know it won't be so easy
this time, but I for one am looking
for another win – especially if we get
an early goal.'

Bobby Cox

DUNDEE FANS partied following the epic victory over Cologne, but on the morning after the night before, the city prepared for a booze policy shake-up. Dundee magistrates held a short private meeting to discuss changes to the city's drinking laws which were due to come into force the following month. The Licensing (Scotland) Act 1962 would place more limits on Dundee's 'dram shops', which used to be under no legal obligation to close at all.

Cologne were also drinking in the last-chance saloon. Their fans decided to boycott their next home game against MSV Duisburg in protest at their team's disappointing display in Dundee.

Only 8,000 Cologne supporters turned up at the Müngersdorfer Stadium, the first time in many years the crowd had been under 16,000. But the first leg result had the opposite effect in Dundee.

Plans to organise a direct 36-seater charter flight from Edinburgh to Cologne were revived. Just ten people had signalled their interest previously, but the 8-1 victory saw that number increase to almost 100 applications for the proposed 'fans' special'.

That meant two or more planes would now be needed, but they would not be taking off from the city's new airstrip despite the Lord Provost's words back in August. Permission to use Riverside Park for a chartered plane was refused. The necessary licence could not be attained in time as there was still certain work to be completed at the airstrip to meet the Ministry of Aviation's conditions. Dundee councillors were told that five gas lamps had to be removed, but the changes would not be completed in time for the proposed flying date of 25 September.

Negotiations then took place with RAF Leuchars in Fife and RNAS Condor in Arbroath to use their airfields as alternative flying venues. This bumped up the proposed cost of the trip and received a lukewarm reception.

A last-minute quotation from Cunard Eagle Airways gave the supporters' club officials renewed hope of success in getting the trip off the ground. The company offered to lay on a charter trip from Dundee for less than £20 per head with hot meals thrown in both ways. The 54-seater plane was to take off from Edinburgh or Renfrew with a bus from Dundee being put on to take the fans to and from the airport.

A stormy meeting was held in the Dundee Supporters' Club's Nethergate clubrooms the Wednesday before the second leg. Postcards were sent out advertising the meeting to the 97 people who were interested.

A representative from Brocklebank, the local Cunard Eagle agents, was invited along to the meeting, but only 47 fans bothered turning up. When the proposal was put to the gathering, only 24 were in favour of accepting the 20-hour round trip. The rest of the supporters objected because they wanted to stay overnight in Cologne instead of coming straight back to Scotland.

The split could not be reconciled because the opposition refused to give in. It would have proved too costly for just 24 fans to go on a 54-seater plane so the whole thing was called off for the second and final time.

Bert McManus from the Dundee Supporters' Club said, 'I'm washing my hands of the whole business. I'm bitterly disappointed at the lack of support, particularly after all the work I've put in and the money I've spent. We had a few other possibilities but they were all too pricey – working out at about £24–25.'

Cunard Eagle Airways didn't leave the Dundee meeting empty-handed, however. Four of the supporters' club officials decided they would go independently on a normal flight and gave their bookings to the Brocklebank representative before leaving.

Dundee kept faith with the V-neck jersey following the European Cup win but the result failed to kick-start their season. Shankly's men were still struggling for domestic form.

They drew their next league match 2-2 against Aberdeen at Dens when a last-gasp Alan Gilzean goal ensured a share of the spoils. Dundee then drew 1-1 against United at Tannadice before a 2-0 home win against newly promoted Clyde provided a much-needed league win before travelling to West Germany.

Dundee fans were fighting over the trip to Cologne at a time that US President John F. Kennedy had declared he would put a man on the moon by the end of the decade. Also preparing to take off to new worlds was Arbroath miniature railway enthusiast Matthew Kerr, who decided to combine his two interests and join the away support. The mini line at West Links was planned and built by Mr Kerr and was an instant hit with the public when it opened in 1935, carrying 11,350 passengers in its first season.

The Dundee fan was making plans to go by train to London, from Dover to Ostend by boat, then the train through Belgium, Holland and Germany to Cologne. 'I've seen the British and French railways working and now this will give me a chance to see the Dutch and German railways, and also see Dundee play Cologne,' he said. 'It's difficult for me to get any summer holidays and this is one trip I'm looking forward to.'

Dundee's success in Europe even prompted fans of their biggest rivals to hitch-hike to West Germany to cheer on the Dark Blues. St Andrews University students Roger Knox, 19, and Alistair Russell, 20, had left Dundee the week before the match to thumb a lift to Dover. Hitch-hiking on the continent wasn't a new experience for them and they intended to get a boat to Calais, a train to Paris, and then hitch-hike again from there to Cologne.

Roger, who spent the summer as a beach leader at Carnoustie, managed to have a word with Cologne assistant secretary Karl Fröhlich about his trip before the first leg. Fröhlich told him that if they managed to get all the way to Cologne that they should get in contact with him and he would get them tickets for the match.

'I hope Dundee win,' said Roger, 'but I'm really a Dundee United supporter.'

United were starting to prosper despite spending the majority of their 53-year existence in the shadow of Dundee. The Tannadice side had done the Dark Blues a massive favour with a shock 1-0 win over Rangers at Ibrox in the 1961/62 title run-in.

Now they made an ultimately abortive attempt to arrange an autumn holiday friendly against Stoke City, whose world famous England international winger

Stanley Matthews remained a star attraction at 47 years of age.

They were, however, more successful with their new floodlighting system, the highest pylon of which was 35 feet higher than those at Dens Park, which reached the 125-foot level.

The giant floodlights would ultimately change the city's skyline, but a much larger construction project would bring a social and economic revolution to Dundee. Project engineer William Fairhurst had just been given a target start date of 31 March 1963 for construction work on the Tay Road Bridge.

Fantastic as it may seem now, plans were once drawn up to build a tunnel under the river between Dundee and Fife before agreement was reached for a bridge. Other proposals included a tube, a causeway with centre span, a high-level bridge from Woodhaven and a low-level bridge with a central span opening for river traffic.

Mr Fairhurst told the first meeting of the Tay Road Bridge Joint Board that the project would be put out to tender in November. He said the bridge should be ready to carry traffic by 1966 at a cost of £4.25 million which, in today's money, would be well over £100 million.

The bridge would usher in a new era of convenience for motorists but would also sound the death knell for the much-loved 'Fifies', the Tay ferries that had transported generations of passengers between Dundee and Newport since 1713. Relationships developed before the first leg at Dens saw insurance inspector Angus Milton head off to West Germany on an all-expenses-paid trip to the return match. While the Cologne team were staying in Dundee, Angus and some of his friends called at the Royal British Hotel in Castle Street hoping to meet their superstars.

The 20-year-old had just finished playing at the Palace Theatre with the City of Dundee Pipe Band and still had a pipe chanter in his pocket. He started to play a few notes and was soon being offered a free trip to Cologne if he would take his pipes and full uniform and perform at the Müngersdorfer before the match. He accepted on the condition he could get time off work. His manager in Edinburgh gave him the green light to pack his suitcase and prompted some last-minute practice on his pipes before the trip.

On Tuesday morning he was due to fly to Cologne on the same plane as the Dundee team, arriving in West Germany that same afternoon.

'I don't know yet what I'll have to do, but the Cologne assistant secretary Karl Fröhlich said I would probably be asked to play at the stadium before the game,' he said. 'There is to be an official reception for the Dundee team and a conducted tour of the city. I believe I'm included in this as well. This will be the first time I've been to Germany. I'll stick to the simple pipe tunes. But I'll manage to work in a bit of "Bonnie Dundee" to cheer the lads on!'

Angus was also hoping to get a seat on the Dundee team bus bringing them home from the airport so that he would make his work on Friday morning.

A request to go by coach was proving popular following the collapse of the charter flight proposal during the heated meeting in Nethergate. A three-day 'Cologne special' was being laid on at short notice by Dundee coach operator Dickson's following a flood of enquiries from supporters. The trip was now being advertised after the Traffic Commissioner granted Dickson's the necessary permission to run a public tour by bus.

The £15 fare included overnight accommodation in Belgium on the outward journey and main meals at Stamford and Wrotham. After the match the

Dundee fans would leave Cologne at midnight and were expected to be back in the city late on Thursday night or early on Friday morning. Admission tickets for the Cologne game were also available at Dickson's and 27 of the 40 seats on the bus had been taken up by the Saturday evening.

Dundee would also receive the support of ten people aged 14–79 who successfully entered the *Sporting Post* 'dream team' competition to win a free trip to Cologne.

Just the day before the players and fans were due to start their journey on Monday evening to West Germany for the second leg on 26 September, there was a tragedy on the route. A Super Constellation airliner on a scheduled flight from Gander airfield in Canada to Frankfurt crashed into the sea 500 miles west of Ireland. The 76 passengers and crew included a company of soldiers who were on their way to a tour of duty in West Germany.

The captain landed the plane on the ocean with such force that seats were uprooted and passengers were propelled forward towards the front of the fuselage. The hull split open and a wing broke off.

Four of the five life rafts were blown away but 51 passengers made it into a 25-man life raft and 48 of them survived. On Monday morning, a Swiss freighter picked them up from the icy water nearly 22 miles from the crash site.

Cologne were also looking for a miracle, but Dundee were travelling to West Germany with a seven-goal lead and a lucky mascot.

The Dundee party left on the first stage of their trip from Dundee West Station and had to run the gauntlet of autograph hunters of all ages. The two oldest supporters waiting for the team were Jeannie Hamilton, 69, and Jessie Mains, 70, who said they were big fans of Dundee defender Ian Ure.

Jeannie said, 'I gave Ian my lucky black cat mascot to take with him. He got it before the first match and look what Dundee did to the Germans. I hope it brings him the same luck this time.'

Cox, Hamilton, Seith, Ure, Penman, Gilzean, Robertson, Brown, Houston and Stuart were all part of the party which left Dundee West Station.

The other four – Bert Slater, Alan Cousin, Bobby Wishart and Gordon Smith – would join up with them in Glasgow.

Slater should have been leaving from Dundee but he realised he had left his passport at home when he turned up for Sunday's final training session. He made a quick dash back to Edinburgh before going on to Glasgow.

Slater asked skipper Bobby Cox to take through his luggage on the train from Dundee. The goalkeeper's luck was out again when Cox forgot he had two bags and left Slater's on the platform! Luckily it was handed in as the train moved off.

Skipper Cox wouldn't be in demand as a luggage attendant, but he stressed he was entirely focused on finishing the job in Germany with a win.

'I know many people in Dundee think we will be beaten in Cologne, although not enough to knock us out,' he said. 'Well, we know it won't be so easy this time, but I for one am looking for another win – especially if we get an early goal.'

Manager Shankly said, 'We're expecting a tough match. Despite that 8-1 defeat, Cologne are no push-over.'

At 8pm that night there was loud cheering in Reform Street as the Dickson's coach set off for West Germany with a Dundee club shield on the window.

The £15-a-head bus trip took off in high spirits carrying 40 Dundee supporters and one Cologne supporter, Anneliese Kroling, a courier with the travel agent. The 22-year-old, who lived in the Hilltown but hailed from Meppen, north of Cologne, climbed aboard the bus waving her Cologne pennant, prompting a chorus of pantomime-style boos from the 50-strong crowd which gathered to see them off.

There had also been pantomime scenes earlier in the day when it turned out that not everyone on the bus was travelling with a passport. Several fans turned up at Dickson's in the afternoon and were sent down to Woolworths where they queued up to use the passport photo machine for two shillings. There was more slapstick when they returned to Dickson's minutes later in a panic after the first coin got jammed and put the machine out of order. The company managed to get on the phone to arrange a last-minute job at Lindsay's photographic shop in Castle Street to save the day.

After an overnight stay in a Glasgow hotel, the Dundee party arrived at Renfrew Airport on Tuesday morning before getting the 10.20am flight to London. The departure lounge was already busy with a mix of boxing fans who were heading to London and Dundee supporters who would be going on to Cologne.

Among those making the trip to West Germany to support Dundee was George 'Lucky' Grant, despite two stellar boxing bouts happening on either side of the Atlantic. Affectionately known as Dundee's 'Mr Boxing', George was born in Princes Street in 1905. He got a job with DC Thomson as a newspaper boy aged just five, selling copies of the *Evening Telegraph* and later *The Courier.*

From these humble beginnings he left school at 14 and worked as a bookmaker's assistant. By the 1930s George had entered the world of boxing promotion, organising Wednesday evening fights at Premierland stadium in William Lane.

He started to organise bigger contests and by 1936 was selling 2,000-plus seats for fights in the Caird Hall. Crowds also flocked to see outdoor shows put on by George at venues such as Dens Park, Dundee Ice Rink and Station Park in Forfar. Around this time he began to become known as 'Lucky' Grant because every time he organised an open-air show he took a risk with the weather but the sun always seemed to shine.

With this background – and his ever-increasing success as a promoter – George became the only Dundonian to have promoted a world-title fight.

He paid the modern-day equivalent of £150,000 to secure a bout between Scot Jackie Paterson and Liverpudlian Joe Curran at Hampden Park, Glasgow in July 1946.

George was now being asked to quote odds on a 'Dundee, Downes, Liston' treble in the departure lounge of the airport from some of the Dundee fans. Terry Downes, the Paddington Express, was facing Sugar Ray Robinson, the Harlem Hep-Cat, one of the greatest fighters in history, five months after losing his title to Paul Pender. The ten-round contest, taking place at Empire Pool, London, was billed as the 'battle of the former middleweight champions'. There was also a much bigger title on the line at Comiskey Park in Chicago where champion Floyd Patterson was the underdog against challenger Sonny Liston.

The Germans were also squaring up to land the top prize when they entered the Tay Road Bridge bidding race the day Dundee flew out to Cologne. William Fairhurst said there was already very keen competition for the contract to build the 8,000-foot four-lane 'wonder'.

He said, 'We should get a lot of tenders. There may be as many as 16 British firms interested, and the Germans are also very interested in the contract.' Mr Fairhurst confirmed the city's Royal Arch would definitely be razed to the ground despite the grand structure being loved by locals and visitors alike.

The Dundee squad arrived in Cologne on Tuesday at 4.30pm after a connecting flight from London and were greeted by a host of young autograph hunters. They were blissfully unaware that the local newspapers had been stirring up trouble.

A misleading photo from the first leg, which appeared to show Alan Cousin punching goalkeeper Fritz Ewert in the face, had been splashed on the front pages.

Ominously, Zlatko Čajkovski, the Cologne team coach, suggested that the result of the return match might be different if the Dundee goalkeeper was injured. 'Maybe in Cologne Dundee lose their goalkeeper and we win 10-0,' he said. The Cologne players also openly talked of revenge.

Alan Gilzean was the first to realise something was wrong.

He spotted the picture in a newspaper in the lounge after the team checked in to their hotel, 15 minutes from the stadium.

One man who knew Cologne's ground well was Dundee United manager Jerry Kerr, who had played there twice, and he gave Shankly advice on what to expect.

'It was in 1946 in the army championships,' said Kerr. 'I played for the 1st Corps and we won both games at Cologne's stadium. It's a magnificent pitch and Dundee need have no worries on that account. The spectators get a long-distance view of the game. There is a remarkable distance from the pitch to the terracing.'

A long tree-lined avenue and spacious parks led up to the 65,000-capacity stadium. At the time it opened in 1923 it was the largest stadium complex in Europe with a cycling track, swimming pools, tennis courts and tracks for various sports. The stadium was included in the green space policy of the city, which reflected the idea of sport in nature and the open air at that time.

Cologne's ground was run by the town council, which received 10% of the gate receipts from each home game. A school of ballet occupied the dressing rooms and indoor gymnasium during the off-season, but such grace appeared to be in short supply elsewhere.

When Dundee finally arrived in Cologne on Tuesday evening they sought out assistant secretary Karl Fröhlich to enquire about training facilities.

Shankly was told that Cologne's stadium belonged to the city and closed at 5pm which meant they would be unable to train under the lights.

The only other available pitch with floodlights was surfaced with red ash. Shankly was told the lights were poor and advised not to go there. Finally, the manager asked about the availability of Cologne's own training ground, but was told that it was also unavailable as it was being used by one of their minor sides.

Shankly and trainer Sammy Kean were having a hard job keeping their emotions in check and it was clear that Cologne were intent on making life as difficult as possible.

'What are these blokes playing at?' said Kean. 'When they were in Dundee they assured us we would be allowed to train at the stadium where the match will be played. If Cologne are being awkward I certainly don't see the point.'

Shankly and Kean cancelled training following the exchange with Fröhlich and instead decided the team would have a short session on the morning of the game.

The dirty tricks had started. Dundee's courage was about to be tested.

They would prove to be up to the fight.

Chapter 5

Sonny Liston,
Sugar Ray Robinson and the
Battle of Cologne

*'It seemed that every British soldier
stationed within a radius of a couple of
hundred miles had come to the game and
swept on to the pitch to defend us.'*

Bobby Cox

COLOGNE WENT into the match in good form
following a 5-2 weekend victory over Wuppertaler
SV which kept them at the top of the table. The
team had also been working on a training ground
routine with reserve goalkeeper Hans Müller in
front of a boarded-up goal which was sectioned and
numbered.

The 1-2-3 sections, on the extreme sides, were the main target areas.

The training stunt wasn't new to the Dundee journalists watching Cologne being put through their paces. The boarded-up goal routine had been a favourite of former Dens Park hero Reggie Smith, who played for Dundee in the wartime league while stationed at RAF Leuchars.

He signed a permanent deal in 1946 and spent two years as a player before returning in a coaching role and was part of back-to-back League Cup victories in 1951 and 1952. He took up the manager's role at Dundee United in 1954, where he introduced the boarded-up goal with suspended numbers from the bar and others propped up on the line.

When he moved to Falkirk in 1957, Smith displayed his sense of humour by having witty comments painted on the framework of the goal.

He branded the top left-hand corner 'Forward's Dream'. Another corner to aim at was titled 'Keepers' Nightmare', while the middle of the goal was marked 'Dead Loss'.

England's European Cup representatives, Ipswich Town, also used the idea at their Portman Road ground.

Ticket sales for the second leg were slow following the first-leg avalanche. The West Germans appeared to be taking more interest in the second leg of the European Cup tie over the border in Brussels between Anderlecht and Real Madrid.

Shankly finally managed to set up a training session the morning before the match, although the team was given no support and the language barrier made things difficult.

Dundee fans started to congregate throughout the morning and gathered at the main station next to the famous Cologne Cathedral. A late rush for tickets meant nearly 40,000 fans were in the stadium before kick-off. These included a few hundred Dundee supporters and a sprinkling of off-duty British servicemen from the Cameronians Regiment. With the Cold War then at its peak they were still stationed in West Germany, nominally part of a post-war British peacekeeping force.

A peace convoy was certainly needed. Cologne were doing everything in their power to ensure Dundee's preparations for the big match were disrupted. Shankly did well to keep his temper in check following another snub before the warm-up.

He asked for the use of four practice balls but Fröhlich brought two to the dressing room and said they were all that he could get.

Dundee directors Jack Swadel and Robert Crichton took their seat in the main stand and claimed to be totally ignored by the Cologne officials. Through a FIFA representative, they attempted to speak to the Cologne president seated beside them, but again they were given the cold shoulder.

If the atmosphere was strained in the directors' box, it was rowdy elsewhere. Every second Cologne fan seemed to have a hunting horn and was making an enormous din.

Shankly named the same side from the first leg but Cologne rang the changes.

Cologne: Schumacher, Pott, Regh, Schnellinger, Wilden, Benthaus, Thielen, Habig, Müller, Schäfer, Hornig.

Dundee: Slater, Hamilton, Cox, Seith, Ure, Wishart, Smith, Penman, Cousin, Gilzean, Robertson.

But it wasn't Cologne's goal that was the centre of attention before the match. The hosts made their intentions clear by sitting an ambulance behind Bert Slater's goal.

Would the dark pre-match hints over an injury to Slater be borne out?

Karl-Heinz Schnellinger, who missed the first leg with injury, returned for Cologne and was given a man-marking job on hat-trick hero Alan Gilzean.

Cologne got off to a great start and very nearly scored straight from the kick-off. Karl-Heinz Thielen beat Bobby Cox and Ian Ure but hooked his shot round the near post from eight yards. Heinz Hornig then struck the Dundee crossbar with a fierce drive on two minutes.

Cologne took the lead on seven minutes from the penalty spot when Alex Hamilton used a hand to push a header by Schäfer over the bar with Slater beaten. Defender Fritz Pott converted from 12 yards but the referee ordered a retake because some of the Cologne players were inside the box before he blew his whistle.

Ernst-Günter Habig stepped up to take the second kick and gave Slater no chance.

Some of the early German tackling was wild, with Gordon Smith and Ure the main victims, although Alan Gilzean also got his fair share of harsh treatment.

The sportsmanship Cologne displayed at Dens had now gone out of the window and they were dishing out the punishment.

Dundee finally created a chance on 22 minutes. A cross by Penman from the right went across the face of goal without any takers.

Tragedy struck for Dundee five minutes later. Slater was badly injured just before the half-hour mark when throwing himself at the feet of Cologne centre-forward Christian Müller.

Slater suffered a deep cut to his ear.

Cologne's ambulance men and club doctor went on the pitch.

They attempted to lead Slater to the waiting ambulance and take him to hospital because they knew Dundee would be down to ten men for the rest of the match. It was a fight they were never going to win. Slater jumped from the stretcher three times after being shoved on to it.

Sammy Kean then signalled he wanted Slater to go to the dressing room for treatment. The dazed goalkeeper was eventually escorted around the Müngersdorfer track by physiotherapist Lawrie Smith and Dundee's 12th man Craig Brown.

After Slater's injury, Shankly stood behind the Dundee goal for about ten minutes, sickened by the tactics of the Cologne forwards. Andy Penman had taken Slater's place between the sticks and Müller immediately scored for Cologne, but the goal was chalked off for a foul on Ure.

Dundee were penned back in their own penalty area and it didn't take long for Cologne to increase their lead just five minutes before the break. Müller hammered a clearance from Ure past Penman at the first time of asking before Hans Schäfer made it 3-0 in first-half injury time.

Shankly was eager to assess Slater's condition at half-time. Dundee were at risk of capitulating and he wanted Slater back out between the sticks for the second half if he was able to carry on. The groggy Slater was bandaged up and received two stitches.

Lawrie Smith had his work cut out on the treatment table while Slater attempted to lift the mood of the fragile dressing room.

He told his team-mates that he now looked like the Hollywood actress Lana Turner, who famously wore a turban in *The Postman Always Rings Twice* in 1946.

The wise-cracking Slater wasn't smiling, however, when Shankly asked him how many fingers he was holding up. The Dundee manager held up four fingers. Slater's answer was three or four out.

Shankly wasn't taking any chances and told Penman he would again be in goal for the second half, but that didn't mean Slater would be taking an early bath. Dundee took to the field after the break with a full complement of players. Slater was put out on the wing to make up the numbers despite being bandaged up and still suffering from concussion.

Hamilton had to lead him on to the pitch and show him where to stand for the kick-off. Slater was finding it difficult to see but just five minutes after the restart he bravely decided to swap jerseys with Penman and go back in goal.

Dundee started to look more solid at the back but the referee was turning a blind eye to some of the rough tackles made by the Cologne players. Müller went clean through on goal on 53 minutes but the courageous Slater got a hand to his shot to push it on to the bar. Slater was the hero again just two minutes later when he threw himself across goal to save a Thielen header from a Müller cross which seemed bound for the top corner.

Cologne did make it 4-0 on 57 minutes. Ure put through his own net while attempting to clear his lines with Slater appearing to have been impeded going up for a cross from the left. Slater and skipper Bobby Cox's appeals to the referee were waved away.

The aggregate score was now 8-5 to Dundee, who were coming under intense pressure. There was further misery on 60 minutes. Dundee conceded a second penalty when Ure brought down Thielen in the box. Several West German officials ran on to the field and Müller aimed a punch at Ure. Habig stepped up to take his second spot kick of the match, but this time he struck the crossbar and Dundee got out of jail.

Dundee's forward line, which was struggling with little service, was rarely in the picture, and only Andy Penman looked capable of pinching a goal.

Cologne were now going route-one with time running out. They were throwing in high balls and hoping to take advantage of the injured Slater. Some of the Dundee players shuddered when they saw how Cologne were going in on him.

The home side were guilty of a number of ugly challenges which went unpunished. There was kicking, punching, spitting and even scratching going on. A

German forward aimed a wild kick at Ure, who responded by sticking the boot into his ribs, but the referee didn't notice because so much was going on elsewhere.

The 40,000 crowd lapped it up and screamed their heads off.

Cologne were now amassing 85% of the possession. On 72 minutes, Dundee almost went five down when a Hornig screamer beat Slater, but Cox managed to clear the ball off the line.

Dundee started to come more into the game in the closing stages and Penman had a chance on 76 minutes to pull a goal back, but screwed wide from seven yards.

Cologne were getting desperate and they appealed for another penalty just eight minutes from time when Alan Gilzean appeared to handle the ball on the 18-yard line. The referee turned down the protests. Cologne were awarded a free kick which came to nothing.

Dundee never gave up, despite what was being thrown at them, although it seemed the game would never finish. They took to kicking the ball as far up the pitch as they could simply to wind down the clock.

The chorus of hate from the Cologne support was increasing by the minute. Then things took a sinister twist with just four minutes to go.

The crowd spilled from the terracing on to the track and right up to the touchline. Police and match officials took no notice but some of Dundee's players had already decided they would make a sprint for it as soon as the final whistle was blown.

The Dundee players were right to get off the field as quickly as possible.

As soon as the final whistle went the team found themselves trapped on the pitch. The crowd poured forward from the touchline with horns blaring. Fists and kicks flew as the Dundee players were swamped in a flood of bodies.

Gilzean took a kick or two on the shins, Cox was struck viciously more than once and the blows also started raining down on Ure, a former boxer. Gordon Smith was left with black and blue legs.

Dundee were saved by the off-duty British Army servicemen who were at the game. The Cameronians Regiment heroes formed a defensive cordon around the players and ushered them to the sanctuary of the dressing room.

Cox suffered a swollen foot and ankle in the free-for-all. He said, 'It was like the relief of Mafeking. It seemed that every British soldier stationed within a radius of a couple of hundred miles had come to the game and swept on to the pitch to defend us. They were in civvies, but you could pick them out by the fearless way they wrapped themselves round us and practically carried us off to safety.'

Slater was the hero of the hour but was struggling to take it all in. He said, 'Even in the second half I got no mercy from the Germans. They kept flailing into me.'

Smith said he was convinced Cologne were out for blood. He said, 'The Germans lost face with their rough methods. They were a good side and had no need to stoop to this level. I have never played against such a team. They resorted to all sorts of shady tricks although they were actually playing well enough without all this.'

Smith described the game as 'the dirtiest in my 22 years in football'. Ure and Hamilton also agreed it was without doubt the dirtiest game they had ever been involved in.

The players were certain they would have lost the tie if Slater hadn't come back on.

Immediately after the game the traditional banquet was laid on in the Cologne clubrooms, but the Dundee directors took the decision to stay away. Having already been snubbed by the Cologne officials, Jack Swadel and Robert Crichton also claimed there had been no direct approach from their hosts to attend the post-match dinner.

There was no way they could stomach sitting down to dinner with the Germans as if nothing had happened after all the disturbing events of the evening. The players and management completely agreed.

Shankly said, 'I have seen plenty of European Cup ties, but nothing like this. I am not overdoing it when I say this was absolutely brutal. Are we supposed to sit back and take all this and not do anything about it?'

The Dundee party instead drove straight back to their hotel in the city.

Cologne assistant secretary Karl Fröhlich said, 'By doing this, Dundee's name will be bad all over Europe. We had a much harder game with Inter Milan but they came along afterwards to eat with us.'

Dundee's players watched highlights of the game on German television back at the hotel before going to bed.

Some Dundee supporters were unaware of what was happening and had turned up outside the Cologne clubrooms after the match expecting to greet the players. The fans instead got an invite to the banquet and ensured the food did not go to waste.

They had a meal and a drink but said they were still given the cold shoulder by Cologne despite staying until midnight to mop up the five-star slap-up fayre laid on. On departure from the banquet, the well-fed and watered Dundee supporters – perhaps protesting somewhat too loudly – said they hadn't enjoyed the experience one bit!

One fan said, 'The atmosphere was terrible and we were certainly glad when we left the clubrooms.' The fact the Germans charged the Dundee fans four marks a head on leaving might have had something to do with the low approval rating for the welcome they received.

Dundee bookie George 'Lucky' Grant wasn't having to put his hand in his pocket, however. The Dark Blues were the odd one out on the 'Dundee, Downes, Liston' treble, although the Battle of Cologne had been as brutal as the blows traded in London or Chicago. Downes defeated Sugar Ray Robinson in ten rounds in London and the five-time champion Robinson was a shadow of his former self in the ring. Robinson was 41 at the time and when asked after the fight how it felt to beat a boxer of such esteem, Downes famously replied, 'I didn't beat Sugar Ray, I beat his ghost.'

On the other side of the Atlantic, Sonny Liston's boast that he'd thrash Floyd Patterson inside five rounds was proved right. Liston pinned Patterson on the ropes in the first round and felled the champion with a series of blows to the head and he was unable to beat the count. It was the first time in history a world heavyweight champion had been knocked out in the first round.

A brash young heavyweight named Cassius Clay – who the Dundee team had met in New York in the summer – invaded the ring at the end of the contest to challenge the new champ. His time would come.

Dundee's time was now.

Despite the brutal encounter, Dundee had booked their place in the draw for the first round. George put that down to the performances of three men in particular.

'Ure was absolutely wonderful,' he said. 'Dundee could have been out of the cup but for him. Slater and Penman were also heroes.'

'Dens men kept cool in a rough house' was the headline in Tommy Gallacher's report in *The Courier*. He praised the team's 'amazing display of courage' and 'their refusal to lose the head at Cologne'.

The West German newspapers which had whipped up so much ill-feeling in the build-up now blamed Dundee for the ugly scenes in Cologne.

The *Cologne Stadt-Anzeiger* said, 'Dundee played against the wall – but Cologne's 4-0 victory wasn't enough. Cologne players were not running, they were racing about the field. They were not shooting, they were bombarding the Scottish goal. Even Dundee's rough play failed to throw Cologne out of their rhythm. Never in their history have Cologne so completely outclassed an opposing team.'

St Andrews University students Roger Knox and Alistair Russell made it to Cologne and witnessed the mayhem at the Müngersdorfer. They intended to return home straight after the match through Ostend in Belgium to get back in time for the opening of the university term on 7 October. But tragedy struck when Roger was involved in a traffic accident in Cologne which left him laid up in hospital with a broken thigh. The former Harris Academy pupil was due to undergo an operation to set the bone which would see him held in West Germany for four or five weeks.

UEFA did nothing to reprimand Cologne for failing to control their fans despite Peco Bauwens of the German Football Association threatening to report it. Bauwens was a former German international who played as a forward before becoming a referee and administrator.

He said, 'We must take some action over these incidents. Why was the crowd allowed to line the touchline with four minutes to go? Where were the police? Why were Dundee players jostled and struck after the final whistle without any protection? Why didn't the referee clamp down on the rough stuff?'

Dundee manager Bob Shankly was angry at the criticism he was getting in some quarters in the wake of the Cologne match. Shankly hit back at accusations that Dundee were 'squealing' too loudly over the treatment they received and should have shown up at the official banquet afterwards. He said Dundee received minimal assistance and no co-operation or friendship from the West Germans from the moment they had arrived in Cologne.

'Make no mistake, Cologne were the superior team on Wednesday,' he said. 'We never got going and I have no complaints about being defeated. But we have every reason to complain about the treatment we got on and off the field. They launched themselves at my players and made no attempt to play the ball. And to suggest we are "cry babies" is utter nonsense.'

Bert Slater went to hospital for an x-ray when the squad returned to Dundee. He was doubtful for the next league match against Rangers, along with Cox, whose ankle was still badly swollen following the battle on the pitch at full time. Penman had picked up a sickness bug in West Germany but was expected to be fit.

Dundee might have been battle-weary, but they won new friends for their conduct.

One man from England was prompted to pick up the quill and doff his cap to the Dundee players for the way they 'kept the head' in the Cologne cauldron. The message arrived at Dens Park from Mr W. Maddick of Plymouth, who said he was writing as 'a humble amateur footballer' who had watched the match against Cologne on TV. He said he wanted to congratulate the Dundee team on showing such great courage and restraint against a team 'with a warped idea of the rules of the game'.

Mr Maddick said he had marvelled at the Dundee players' self-control. 'I want to thank you for setting an example to somewhat hot-headed players like myself,' he said.

Anderlecht put five-time winners Real Madrid to the sword at the Heysel Stadium in Brussels with a 1-0 home win to go through 4-3 on aggregate. The early exit of the Spanish champions along with Cologne – both among the favourites to win the competition – had thrown the tournament wide open. The Spanish press had the knives out for Real when they returned to Madrid.

The scoring feats of AC Milan, who were 14-0 aggregate winners over Union Luxembourg, and Ipswich Town, who racked up a 14-1 total against Floriana of Malta, certainly caught the eye in the preliminary round, despite the standard of opposition.

Dundee's result against one of the early favourites had also made Europe stand up and take notice.

AC Milan, Anderlecht, Benfica, Dukla Prague, Feyenoord, Galatasaray, Ipswich Town and Sporting Lisbon joined Dundee among the 16 teams in the first-round draw. They might have snubbed the West

German banquet, but Dundee were now dining with Europe's elite.

First it was back to the bread and butter of the Scottish First Division.

Chapter 6

Tall Ships Go

*'We should be able to play our usual game
and show everyone that we are not the
"dirty team" some continentals appear to
have branded us.'*

Bob Shankly

TITLE-WINNING HERO Pat Liney was back in
goal when Dundee returned to league action against
in-form Rangers at Ibrox just three days after the
Battle of Cologne. Rangers were top of the league
after scoring 11 goals in their first four games following
victories against St Mirren, Celtic, Partick Thistle and
Hibernian.

Scot Symon's side had also been in the wars
midweek. Rangers had just returned from the Battle of

Seville, the second leg of their European Cup Winners' Cup tie in Spain, where all hell broke loose.

Rangers had won the first leg 4-0 at Ibrox and the Spaniards were out for revenge. John Greig, Davie Wilson, Bobby Shearer, Ronnie McKinnon and Jim Baxter were all targeted by Seville's hatchet men. Rangers went through 4-2 on aggregate but manager Symon said he had never seen 'such disgusting scenes of violence and brutality'.

Now battle-weary Rangers and Dundee shared the spoils. Rangers fought back for a point despite going behind when Hugh Robertson's shot was deflected past Rangers goalkeeper Billy Ritchie by Bobby Shearer's leg.

The European Cup draw on 2 October would provide a welcome distraction from the domestic struggles. Dundee were paired with Portuguese cracks Sporting Lisbon.

The famous green-and-white hoops had qualified for the European Cup after winning their domestic title for the first time in four years. They played 26 games, winning 19, losing two, drawing five and scoring 66 goals to finish two points ahead of FC Porto and seven ahead of European champions Benfica.

Renowned as one of the toughest defensive teams in Europe, Sporting had given up only 17 goals in the title-winning season. There were eight international players in their ranks and midfielder Fernando Mendes was the most capped player in the side with 12 appearances for Portugal.

The domestic season in Portugal would not start until 21 October but Sporting showed no signs of ring rust when they defeated League of Ireland side Shelbourne 7-1 on aggregate in the preliminary round.

Sporting also proved themselves to be worthy ambassadors for their country when the Shelbourne players were given silver cigarette boxes as a gift at the after-match dinner.

Shankly said, 'I think it is a very good draw for us. Sporting must be a very good side – you only need to look at their record to know that. We are not the least perturbed about playing the first leg away from home.

'As a matter of fact, in view of what happened in Cologne, it may even be a good thing. This way we will go to Lisbon on level terms. We should be able to play our usual game and show everyone that we are not the "dirty team" some continentals appear to have branded us.'

Dundee had journeyed to most European countries in the past but the trip to Portugal for the first leg on 24 October would be breaking new ground.

A national rail strike in protest at Dr Richard Beeching's proposed cuts to the network brought the UK to a halt a day after the European Cup draw was made. That meant disruption for England fans travelling to watch the European Championship qualifier against France at Sheffield Wednesday's Hillsborough ground.

Walter Winterbottom had been in charge when England thrashed Portugal 10-0 in Lisbon in 1947 to gain the accolade 'Lions of Lisbon'. The England manager was now asked about Dundee's chances of overcoming another difficult assignment against Sporting in Lisbon.

He said, 'I've seen Sporting Club play once or twice. They're fast, accurate and most progressive in style. Like Benfica they can switch over to Iron Curtain-type defence in an instant.'

Francisco Santos, the London correspondent of two Portuguese newspapers, said Dundee could expect a visit from Sporting administrative manager Armando Ferreira, who worked closely with the head coach and liked to weigh up unknown opposition.

'They are very good in defence,' he said. 'But shooting for goal is a big weakness and they were very poor in Ireland in the game with Shelbourne.'

Andy Lothian was also set to bring the biggest names in pop to the city when he unveiled plans to turn a new club into 'Dundee's top pop spot'. Mr Lothian, who ran the popular Tomb Jazz Club, started up the Top Ten Club at the Palais Ballroom and vowed to attract the UK's top pop stars and bands to perform.

Guest stars booked to appear at the Tay Street venue for the first show on 14 October were Emile Ford and the Checkmates, Robby Hood and his Merrie Men, Johnny Washington, Johnny Hudson and the Hi-Four, and Clint and the Tornadoes.

One entertainer who was already appearing in Dundee was Canadian harmonica virtuoso Tommy Reilly, who was starting a fortnight's run at the Palace Theatre. He composed and played the music for the soundtracks of many movies and well-known TV series including *Dixon of Dock Green* and *The Navy Lark*.

But there was a TV blackout for one virtuoso performance which took place in Lisbon in the build-up to Dundee's European Cup match. The world's two greatest players were facing each other in the Intercontinental

Cup between the winners of the European Cup and the South American Copa Libertadores.

Eusébio and Pelé seldom had the chance to meet in a competitive match but now their paths crossed over two legs to determine the undisputed kings of club football. Santos won the first leg 3-2 at the Maracanã in September but the return match in Lisbon on 11 October was considered the greatest performance of Pelé's career.

He orchestrated a rout and scored a hat-trick in a 5-2 win watched by 73,000 fans, but there was a worldwide ban on the game being shown anywhere but Portugal. Benfica had turned down the chance to permit the match to be televised outside the country. It angered many people, including European football's governing body.

Just days later, the *Unicorn*'s half-mile voyage downriver, the first in 89 years, similarly captured the imagination of the Dundee public. In an intricate operation, the ship was hauled off the bank of mud it lay on at Earl Grey Dock then escorted out on to the river by two tugs.

The 46-gun wooden frigate once again felt the ripple of water past her sides as she gracefully moved to make way for the building of the Tay Road Bridge. Twenty thousand people turned out along the riverfront on 13 October while hundreds perched atop piles of timber and watched from the roofs of buildings.

Back at Dens Park, Pat Liney, Dundee's ever-present goalkeeper in their title-winning season, was prepared to rock the boat to get a move. Liney played against Rangers but was again second choice following Bert Slater's return from injury.

Unhappy to be back on the sidelines, Liney approached Shankly after training and made a verbal request for a move. It was immediately turned down. Later in the day he followed up with a registered letter addressed to the directors, reiterating his desire to move away from Dens Park.

'I understand the club's viewpoint all right – the boss has explained it to me,' said Liney. 'But I've had only one game in the last month and that was against Rangers at Ibrox a fortnight ago in the first team. I'm not kidding myself that being out of the first team has no bearing on how I feel now, but I didn't feel so bad about it as long as I was playing regularly in the reserves. I just don't see any future for me at Dens with Bert Slater available for the league side and young Alistair Donaldson for the reserves.'

Liney was the second player to request a transfer in 24 hours following an earlier demand submitted by reserve defender George Ryden. Shankly stressed Liney and Ryden would be staying put.

'This is the first time since I came here that I have been happy about the goalkeeping situation,' said Shankly. 'If Pat has sent a letter, it will be left to me to deal with, and Pat won't get away, although I sympathise with his position.'

Likewise, Andy Penman's request for a move earlier in the season had been turned down by Shankly, who kept him in the first team. His return to form had been like a new signing for the club.

Penman withdrew his transfer request after the home fans sung his praises during the 2-1 victory against Dundee United in the League Cup group stages.

'A good ticking off from the manager restored my confidence and form,' said Penman. 'I proved to myself that I could still do it and since then my confidence has come on greatly. I feel my game is getting slightly better.

'I know the crowds were against me in a number of games, but that did not affect me. My father gave me the best advice in football. He said, "Never worry about having a bad game … just try to do better next time.'"

Shankly also boosted his squad with the signing of 17-year-old defender Tom Cargill from Arbroath Lads' Club. Cargill owed his provisional signing to a decent match for Dundee reserves against Falkirk at Brockville and the fact that his father was a Dundee supporter.

The teenager had an offer to sign for Leeds United following a visit to Elland Road but decided to stay at home in Arbroath where he was an apprentice joiner at his dad's business. His father, who was a renowned junior player in his younger days, was thrilled when Shankly made his approach. Cargill was immediately farmed out to Blairgowrie Juniors to gain further experience.

Dickson's were planning to embark on a slightly longer journey, with plans to run a bus to Portugal for the first leg. Owner Robert Dickson said one or two people had already expressed an interest in the trip which he predicted would last 'seven or eight days'. Arrangements were still being made but he said the trip would likely cost £35 to £40, including an overnight stay in Paris on the return journey.

Dundee's spy in the camp was Brodie Lennox, who would at least be one voice shouting for the team in Lisbon if the bus trip didn't get off the ground. The former Scottish amateur golf star was running a guest house in Estoril, the famous golf resort situated some 15 miles from the Portuguese capital. His family-run hotel, The Lennox, was in the heart of town with tartan draping the walls, golf balls dangling from the ceiling of the bar, and trophies all over the house.

Late summer had given way to autumn as Dundee rediscovered their form ahead of the first leg in Lisbon. They followed up the 1-1 draw with Rangers by taking three points from the next two games. Falkirk were defeated 2-1 at Dens before a 2-2 away draw with Hibs.

Up next for Dundee was a home match against Kilmarnock where it was rumoured a Sporting Lisbon representative would be in attendance to run the rule over their opponents.

The *Sporting Post* had been tipped off that he had arrived in the city the night before the match. But, despite countless efforts, they could not find him. Charlie Keith regularly popped into the office for a chat on Saturday mornings before returning in the afternoon to help make up the league tables. On this particular weekend, he did so again.

As he was popping out for lunch, Mr Keith was asked, somewhat tongue-in-cheek, 'If you see a Sporting Club Lisbon director out there, just bring him into the office.'

He returned ten minutes later with a tall, impeccably-dressed man, and introduced him as the Sporting Lisbon administrative manager Armando Ferreira.

'How did you manage that?' he was asked by the sports editor.

'Ach, I'd just left this office and was wandering down Reform Street,' replied Mr Keith. 'I saw this man looking in a shop window and, remembering what you had just said, I thought: "He's certainly not from Dundee." I just asked him if he was from Sporting Club Lisbon and he said "yes". I then told him the local newspaper wanted to speak to him and he agreed to come in.'

Forty-two-year-old Ferreira was a former Sporting Lisbon player who won the league five times and had five caps for Portugal. He arrived in Dundee to make preparations for the away leg and to offer the hand of friendship to his club's European Cup opponents.

'We heard about the rough treatment Dundee got in Cologne but there will be none of that in Lisbon,' he said. 'We are not a dirty team and we hope for two good, clean games.'

Ferreira said they had heard very little about Dundee but had a great respect for Scottish football. He remembered watching Scotland play Portugal in Lisbon back in 1950 in a 2-2 draw where he was impressed by George Young and Billy Steel. Steel was still playing for Derby County at the time before he became a legendary figure at Dundee where he was instrumental in their two League Cup successes.

Ferreira spoke to Shankly about training facilities during his visit and made arrangements for his team to stay at the Queen's Hotel for the second leg.

He took his seat in the stand and watched Dundee defeat Kilmarnock 1-0 and move to within four points of league leaders Hearts despite being without Hamilton and Ure, both on international duty for Scotland in Cardiff. The duo helped Scotland to a 3-2 win against Wales in the British Home Championship at a time when club games didn't stop for international matches.

Ure was 'proud as punch' after swapping shirts with his hero John Charles at full time while Hamilton was just as delighted about his exchange with right-back Stewart Williams. Charles had just returned to English football with Leeds United following a five-year spell in Italy with Juventus where he became a flag bearer for Anglo–Italian relations. He scored 93 goals in 150 Serie A games and was twice named Italy's footballer of the year as Juventus won three league titles and two Italian Cups.

The Gentle Giant was not the first British player to make an impact in Italy. In fact, a former Dundee player was among the early pioneers.

Peter Cabrelli, who was born in Dundee in 1910, was the son of Italian exile Andrew Cabrelli, who began the family fish and chip business with shops in Hilltown and Lawton Road. He started his career in the junior ranks before signing for Dundee in 1930 but never managed to break into the first team. He joined Forfar Athletic and, during this spell, also played in matches for Borgotaro, Genoa and Inter Milan while in Italy to visit family.

Cabrelli was still a part-time footballer when he was offered professional terms as player-coach with Inter Milan. However, he turned down the move to Serie A due to commitments at his dad's chippy in Dundee.

He eventually went on to sign a full-time deal with Falkirk before joining Raith Rovers until the outbreak of the Second World War when he was called up for military service. While stationed as a driver with the army in England, he guested for various teams including Arsenal, Crystal Palace, Bradford City, Millwall and Reading.

Following the defeat of Nazi Germany, he turned out for Dundee United only to hit the headlines for the wrong reasons when he and Dundee's Kinnaird Ouchterlonie were sent off for fighting during the local derby in January 1946.

His career wound down with spells at Arbroath and Montrose before he retired in 1948. But fittingly for a man with so many links to Italy, he continued to play well into his 40s for the appropriately named Dundee Juventus in the local Half-Holiday League.

Cabrelli might have left Dens after a short spell but the club remained in his heart. When he went into the family business he had a custom-made stained glass mural hung behind the frying pans. It was a scene from Dens Park during a game and Cabrelli was one of the players.

Cabrelli's beloved Dundee were now on a seven-game unbeaten run. Ferreira left by train for Edinburgh immediately after the Kilmarnock game and didn't have time to stop off for a bag of chips from Cabrelli's shop at the top of Caird Avenue. The Sporting representative flew home to Lisbon via London and Paris. Dundee would face a similar journey to get to Portugal from Renfrew.

Shankly, director Robert Crichton, trainer Sammy Kean, physio Lawrie Smith, Bobby Cox, Bobby Seith, Hugh Robertson and Alex Stuart left Tay Bridge Station for Glasgow on Sunday night. Robertson had taken a kick above the ankle against Kilmarnock and was limping but Shankly was confident he would still be able to start Wednesday's game. The party was joined in Glasgow by Slater, Wishart, Smith, Penman, Cousin, Gilzean, Houston and Brown.

The Dundee officials said they were impressed with Ferreira, who had made it clear that the Portuguese would do everything to help the Dark Blues. They were told they could train any time they wanted once they arrived in Lisbon and a bus would be put on for them.

Dundee were due to fly from Renfrew at 10.20 the following morning.

A technical error delayed take-off by two hours so they had to skip lunch at the first stop, London Airport, in order to make their connection to Paris.

The squad was joined in London by Ure and Hamilton. Both were threatening to turn out at Dundee's first training stint in Portugal wearing the Welsh jerseys they picked up in Cardiff. Hamilton, though, was struggling to make Wednesday's game. The right-back had recovered from a knock on his right leg against Wales but when he woke up the next morning he was experiencing pain from a strained thigh muscle in his left leg.

He still thought his chances of starting in Lisbon were good. Craig Brown would come in at right-back if he didn't make it.

The Dark Blues left from Paris for Lisbon with the world on the brink of nuclear war after American President John F. Kennedy blockaded Cuba to stop the communist build-up. The Soviet Union had secretly stationed nuclear weapons on the island, aimed at the US mainland only 100 miles away. When the US discovered them and demanded their withdrawal, there ensued the most dangerous confrontation of the entire Cold War. America and the Soviet Union went head to head in a perilous game of brinksmanship. People throughout the world were terrified that a nuclear holocaust was just days away.

A weary and hungry Dundee party finally arrived in Lisbon at 6.45pm looking like they'd just emerged from a fall-out shelter.

The players had only had a cup of coffee and two small sandwiches since 8am after missing their lunch in London.

They were welcomed by Sporting officials and a crowd of reporters, photographers and Portuguese fans. A green-and-white club bus was put at Dundee's disposal with a colourful array of pennants from Sporting's past opponents hanging from the roof. The Dark Blues were taken to the 11-storey Embaixador Hotel which had a shower and bath in every room, a nightclub, and a sun parlour on the roof.

The famished players had a late meal on the ninth floor, where they left the hotel staff in no doubt about how hungry they were. They wolfed down no fewer than ten dozen buttered hard rolls before the soup arrived. Before that, at manager Shankly's behest, Sammy Kean had carefully scrutinised the menu, indicating what was appropriate with a suitable emphasis on ham and eggs, and steak and chips. Nothing too fancy – more a case of plain and plenty!

Physio Smith also had his instructions and had come armed with pills, pellets and powders to counteract various contingencies. Several players had fallen ill when Shankly was in charge of Falkirk's tour of Israel in 1953. The Dens boss blamed the strangely cooked food and water and, although accepting that Lisbon was now becoming a popular tourist destination, he was determined there would be no repeat.

The players then journeyed the three miles from their central hotel to the stadium to check out the pitch and the Portuguese floodlight system.

Dundee arrived to find the stadium was guarded by a number of Great Danes which Sporting kept as pets. The dogs ate 6lb of meat a day and had become their unofficial mascots.

The floodlight system contained 260 lamps which mounted on pylons on one side of the ground only. The rest were on the stand roof.

Two of Dundee's own leading lights – Alex Hamilton and Hugh Robertson – went off and received treatment for their injuries at the stadium from the Sporting masseurs.

The team had no complaints about the pitch, which was firm and level. The hosts were rolling out the red carpet and giving Dundee the VIP treatment. They were also shown around the stadium, which had over 100 rooms connected with every sport under the sun. There was even a special room for chess players.

There were no plans to train until the following day at 5pm to avoid the heat.

Shankly said, 'We'll be taking it easy this time. We never worked so hard as before the Cologne game and we're still in great shape. If the margin is two goals I'll be happy. That's either way.'

Shankly was delighted with the welcome but cancelled a sightseeing tour of the city which had been arranged by the Portuguese officials for the following day. He felt his players had done enough travelling for the time being.

Dundee's players took a slightly shorter journey after Monday's endeavours. Despite struggling with the heat, some went shopping locally. A few others headed 15 miles up the coast to Estoril, which Bobby Cox described as fabulous.

'Emblemie' was one word the Dundee players kept hearing in Lisbon.

Smiling faces expressed the message by mouth. Hands indicated they would like a Dundee pin badge. The players wished they had taken more to repay the hospitality.

One Sporting fan was so desperate for a Dundee badge as a souvenir that he offered up his overcoat to squad player Alex Stuart in exchange for it!

The players returned to the stadium for training at 5pm.

Left-winger Robertson had recovered well and was looking certain to play.

He stayed on following the session to be treated by Lawrie Smith. Doug Houston would replace him in attack if he was unable to start.

The team was asked back to the stadium afterwards to watch an international athletics meeting between Portugal and Argentina, which didn't start until 10pm. The players were allowed to stay up late to watch the track action with an extra sleep session scheduled for the following day.

Some of the players were disappointed there was no bullfighting in Lisbon but they enjoyed some good sprinting at the athletics event despite a ghostly atmosphere with only 2,500 people present at the 60,000-capacity stadium.

The Wednesday morning of the game saw Dundee training from 10.30am until lunchtime. Hamilton was passed fit after his leg strain but Robertson broke down before kick-off, which meant Shankly would be unable to field the same side that beat Cologne. Houston would start, despite only having played four league and cup games for Dundee.

Lunch was the last square meal before the match. The players went to bed in the afternoon to get some rest and rise fresh for the game, which would be kicking off at 10.45pm British time because of the heat. A pre-match siesta was customary for players in Portugal but this was something different for Dundee. Ian Ure was unconvinced he would enjoy his afternoon sleep.

'I don't really like the idea of sleeping in the daytime,' he said. 'I have done it before and found I never played well after it.'

In the days before there was such a thing as a European scouting system, Dundee got information on their 'unknown' opponents from a variety of sources, whether they be a British embassy official or a former golfer-turned-B&B owner in Estoril. They knew little about the team they were facing.

Sporting had warmed up for the match with a 5-3 friendly win against Atlético Clube de Portugal. They put off naming their starting line-up owing to doubts over the fitness of 23-year-old Mário Lino, rated the best right-back in Portugal. He was eventually replaced by Portugal international defender José Carlos, while South African-born David Júlio was recalled to complete the midfield.

There was also a change of referee with Henri Faucheux of France taking charge instead of the Norwegian official who was expected to handle the match. The Dundee players woke from their afternoon slumber in time to prepare for kick-off, while back at home, many of their fans stayed up late to listen to the game on shortwave radio.

Sporting: Carvalho, Carlos, Hilário, Pérides, Lúcio, Júlio, Hugo, Osvaldo, Mascarenhas, Geo, Morais.

Dundee: Slater, Hamilton, Cox, Seith, Ure, Wishart, Smith, Penman, Cousin, Gilzean, Houston.

A crowd of almost 50,000 welcomed both teams and kick-off was delayed for five minutes while the teams swapped pennants and posed for photos.

Several hundred police officers patrolled the track but within two minutes there was a pitch invasion. Hundreds of spectators from the home support broke out from the terracing on the far side and on to the track, 15 yards from the pitch. The police were happy to keep them on the outside of the running track although the Dundee players could have been excused for feeling a little anxious after Cologne.

The game was end-to-end from the very start.

Dundee almost went behind when Sporting danger man Mascarenhas took the ball inside Hamilton, but winger João Morais shot wildly over the bar from 12 yards.

Penman put Gilzean through one-on-one with the goalkeeper on seven minutes but the inside-left overran the ball and Joaquim Carvalho collected.

Inside-right Geo struck the side netting after a poor clearance from Ure.

Sporting were gaining momentum and Slater was forced to pull off a great save from José Pérides after Wishart failed to clear his lines.

Slater was then called upon to pull off a vital stop from Osvaldo Silva. The Dundee defence was struggling under the mounting pressure.

There was some let-up when Gilzean had another chance to put Dundee ahead following a slip from Penman, but his 20-yard shot went wide. Houston was next to put the Sporting defence to the test with another strike from distance but it was aimed straight at goalkeeper Carvalho.

On 26 minutes, Wishart charged up the field after taking the ball out of defence before hitting a snarling drive from 30 yards out which was pushed past the post. Houston and Gilzean then combined to test Carvalho and force another corner before play was stopped on 33 minutes when a dog invaded the pitch. Pitch invasions of all sorts were becoming a feature of Dundee's European Cup run.

Silva forced a good stop from Slater on 40 minutes but Dundee could have gone ahead after Gilzean split the Sporting defence open with a 30-yard pass. Penman's effort was just wide but it gave Dundee confidence as they went in level.

Dundee were quickly out of the blocks following the restart. Carvalho was the busier goalkeeper and strikes by Cousin, Penman and Smith forced three corners in the space of as many minutes.

Sporting hit back strongly and Slater proved why he was Dundee's number one when he threw himself bravely at the feet of Mascarenhas to stop a certain goal.

The pendulum swung backwards and forwards. Gilzean was given another chance to strike a blow for Dundee but he shot wide on 56 minutes.

Ure was in commanding form at the back despite the tidal wave of attacks while Houston was running himself into the ground in his first European start. The young Glaswegian didn't look out of place among such distinguished company on the biggest stage in club football and he was chasing every lost cause.

On 60 minutes the referee turned down a penalty claim for Sporting when Cox appeared to block a shot inside the box from Silva with his arm. Slater saved a long-range Júlio strike on 64 minutes before diving at the feet of Hugo from six yards out just minutes later to keep the scores level.

It was now backs-to-the-wall defending.

On 73 minutes Ure cleared off the line from Morais with Slater beaten. The big defender was the hero again when Júlio's goal-bound effort struck him full in the face and rebounded to safety.

Slater again kept Sporting at bay with a save at the near post from Geo. It looked like Dundee would hold on, before tragedy struck with 90 seconds to go.

Slater punched a high cross from the right into the path of Geo, who struck the ball back towards the near post. Slater recovered and tipped it on to the bar before Wishart booted it off the line.

The referee signalled a goal despite Dundee protests. It prompted hundreds of soft cushion seats to be thrown on to the running track from the high terracing above by the jubilant Sporting fans.

The Courier's Tommy Gallacher wired back and described the Sporting match as 'one of the fastest, most gruelling but sportiest European Cup ties ever seen'.

After the match, Mascarenhas, the Sporting forward who had spent two years at Benfica, said Dundee's defence was one of the best he had ever come up against. He reserved special praise for Ure, whose reputation was growing throughout Europe.

'He has got everything and in particular a great positional sense,' he said. 'Ure overshadowed me completely, but I will do much better at Dundee. The Scottish champions must play the attacking game. I think this will present us with a better chance to score goals. They will open their defence for us.'

Gordon Smith said Sporting played better than the Benfica team he faced two years ago in the European Cup when he was with Hearts.

Smith himself was the subject of high praise in return from full-back Hilário, who had once marked the great Brazilian winger Garrincha out of a game. 'Smith was wonderful,' he said.

David Júlio agreed about Smith's abilities, describing how the Scot would backtrack to cover in defence as well as being creative further forward. 'He goes back, back all the time,' he said. 'When we go in for the ball we get plenty of trouble.'

Among the 50,000 crowd at the Estádio José Alvalade were Arbroath miniature railway proprietor Matthew Kerr and former Aberdeen footballer Lachie McMillan. Mr Kerr flew to Lisbon on the night of the match and said he would be staying on in Portugal to make a study of their railways and old engines.

McMillan, who was in Lisbon on holiday, was best remembered for his bravery at Dens Park after he broke his leg in a cup tie against Dundee in 1931. That day he refused to leave the field despite the extent of the injury and kept stamping his feet on the ground, saying, 'Ach, it'll come all right in a wee while.' The physio was forced to drag McMillan off the pitch. He fainted inside the dressing room and remained unconscious until he woke up in hospital!

Now, as a belated token of his appreciation, he had provided his support to Dundee in a break from the sunbed.

Dundee went to the after-match banquet in a city centre hotel where the players were in confident mood despite losing the match at the death. They firmly believed they would win the second leg and go through to the next round. Shankly and Kean were also making positive noises.

The party finally got to bed at 3am but were up again at 9am, ready for the lengthy trip home via Madrid, London and Edinburgh. They got to London half an hour late following a delay from Portugal which meant the Edinburgh trio of Smith, Wishart and Slater missed their connection.

The rest of the group flew to Renfrew and arrived back in the city around midnight, where Shankly warned there was still work to do if Dundee were to advance.

'They are still a very good side and we'll have a tough job on our hands next week,' he said. 'I thought we could win after the first 15 minutes on Wednesday as our breakaways were always dangerous. I wasn't disappointed with the result but I thought it was a pity to lose by such an unsatisfactory goal.'

The fighting spirit of Lachie McMillan would be needed for the second leg.

Chapter 7

Taming the Lions of Lisbon

'Dundee will win the cup. Nothing else can
happen as long as they have Smith.'

Sporting Lisbon president,
Commodore Joel Pascoal

THERE WAS massive relief when the Cuba crisis
was finally defused. Soviet premier Nikita Khrushchev
backed down and the Soviet nuclear missiles in Cuba
were disassembled. In return, President John F.
Kennedy abandoned the USA's own missile sites in
Turkey. The most hostile period in US–Soviet relations
since World War Two was now at an end.

A difference of opinion between Dundee and
Sporting Lisbon concerning a possible deciding fixture
was also settled amicably.

It seems almost remarkable now that there was once an era when the likes of extra time and penalties didn't exist in football.

Both clubs eventually agreed that a third game would be played in Paris if they failed to settle their European Cup tie at Dens on Wednesday, 31 October. The date of 28 November had previously been agreed but sorting out the venue proved more problematic.

Initially Sporting wanted to fix up Real Madrid's Bernabeu for a replay, while Dundee's first choice was London. Paris was the alternative suggested by the Dark Blues. The problem was eventually settled without drawing straws or duelling pistols because the French capital was also the second choice of the Portuguese champions. It was just as well because Dundee were prepared to refer the matter to the European Cup committee if agreement could not be reached.

There was only one casualty from the first leg in Lisbon. Doug Houston injured his knee during the match, having replaced Hugh Robertson in the starting line-up. In the event, Houston was fit enough to feature in Dundee's next game, a 2-0 league defeat at East End Park against Jock Stein's Dunfermline, who would also be in European action on Wednesday.

Sporting Lisbon's return to domestic duty against Leixões, 24 hours later on Sunday evening, was just as disappointing when they suffered a 1-0 defeat.

Osvaldo Silva, Sporting's attacking midfielder from Brazil, said it would be a different story against Dundee. He said, 'Sporting is one of the greatest clubs in Europe and every time I play for them I feel the enormous responsibility of being one of the "Lions". It was this responsibility I felt last Wednesday when I played against Dundee. This is the second time Sporting have tried to enter the quarter-finals of this competition. This time we will make it – I am almost sure.

'Last Wednesday's match was fantastic. A penalty could have been given to us when I was brought down by Ian Ure, but all credit must be paid to the strong Scottish defence. Ure is an extraordinary player. The outside-right, the two inside-forwards and the left-half are also very good. The whole team is powerful and it is no wonder we couldn't score more than one goal.

'I know that in football anything can happen. We could be defeated by two, three or four goals. But we could also score one, and if we do that in the first half, the tie will be ours. We don't believe in playing defensive football – we will attack.'

A squad of 16 players from Sporting started the long journey from Lisbon to Dundee on Monday morning following the Leixões defeat. They would go via Paris, London and Edinburgh and were due to be met by Bob Shankly, Sammy Kean and Lawrie Smith on their arrival at Turnhouse Airport.

José Périeés was declared unfit after pulling a muscle and didn't make the plane to Scotland, but right-back Mário Lino was recalled after missing the first leg. Ernesto Figueiredo was also expected to start.

Sporting head coach Julio Pereira, better known as Juca, said he was very disappointed with his team's display against Leixões. He put some of the blame for the defeat down to his side losing their concentration after the Leixões centre-forward broke his leg in the early exchanges. The injury reduced their opponents to ten men for almost the entire game but it was particularly distressing for the Sporting players as he was a former team-mate.

'They didn't live up to their name and fight like Lions,' he said. 'But the early leg break had an upsetting effect. We were playing against ten men for 87 minutes but some of our players didn't fight as they should have.'

Juca started life as a goalkeeper before being converted to a midfielder. He joined Sporting in 1949 and played in 178 league and cup games for the club, winning five Portuguese titles and collecting six caps for Portugal. He retired at the age of 29 in 1958 following a knee injury before becoming the youngest manager to win the Portuguese title, leading Sporting to glory in the 1961/62 season.

Juca, who was promoted from the under-19s to the top job, said he had told his players that their task at Dens would call for 100% effort from the first to the last.

David Júlio, who had broken his right leg the previous season, said the Leixões player's injury had badly affected the team's mentality on Sunday.

'The accident in the early minutes concerned our players very much and they never stuck to their usual game,' he said. He was expecting a 'good clean game' at Dens but stressed 'Dundee will go out for the kill' in their bid for a quarter-final place.

Júlio was one of the first South Africans to ply his trade in European club football after being spotted playing for Mozambique side Lourenco Marques in 1956. Sporting offered him a contract and his friends and team-mates in the Transvaal League raised enough money to get him to Portugal to sign a deal. He was generally looked upon as a pioneer for South African football overseas.

The Portuguese party took almost 13 hours to get to Dundee and they arrived at the city's Queen's Hotel in Perth Road just before midnight. The Sporting players spent the next day sleeping off any jet lag after enjoying a lie-in. They finally left their hotel at 10.30am in driving rain to go round the Dundee shops. Most of them were looking for Scottish souvenirs to take home.

Club president Joel Pascoal, a retired naval commodore, said the team were not taking the colder weather too badly since it resembled a Portuguese winter. Commodore Pascoal was a self-confessed 'old salt' who was used to the driving rain and had not long left a naval career spanning 40 years.

'It's a long road to Tipperary and Dundee too,' he said. 'We were scheduled to fly out at 8.30am but some technical trouble with the aircraft delayed us until 10.45am. Then we could not land as planned at Turnhouse because of a wind difficulty. The weather is fine, as long as it stays like this.'

It's Dundee's League: Alan Gilzean scores Dundee's second goal in the 3-0 win against St Johnstone which clinched the title in 1962 (DC Thomson)

Field of Dreams: Dens Park pictured in July 1962 after new terracing was put in place with Dundee Law in the background (DC Thomson)

*Heroes of the Hour: The Dundee squad
are pictured ahead of the 1962/63
season proudly displaying the league
championship trophy
Back Row, Left to Right: Gordon
Smith, Andy Penman, Bobby Seith,
Alex Stuart, Pat Liney, Bobby Wishart,
Craig Brown, Bobby Waddell, Lawrie
Smith (physiotherapist), Alan Gilzean
and Ian Ure. Front Row, Left to
Right: Sammy Kean (trainer), Alex
Hamilton, Jack Swadel (director),
Bobby Cox, James Gellatly (chairman),
Alan Cousin, Bob Crichton (director),
Hugh Robertson and Bob Shankly
(manager). (DC Thomson)*

*Calm before the storm: Cologne
assistant secretary Karl Fröhlich and
Dundee boss Bob Shankly meeting at
Dens before the first leg (Fotopress/
Dave Martin)*

Breaking new ground: Cologne manager Zlatko Čajkovski alongside his players as they line up at Glenesk Park for a training session (DC Thomson).

Rain check: Zlatko Čajkovski examines the Dens Park pitch following the tropical weather in Dundee watched by Anton Regh (left) and Karl-Heinz Ripkens (DC Thomson).

Out Cold: Cologne goalkeeper Fritz Ewert lies sparked out in his goalmouth following the accidental clash with Alan Cousin in the opening minutes. (DC Thomson)

King of Dens Park: Alan Gilzean doing what he does best as he scores with a header against Cologne during the 8-1 rout which left the German Embassy reeling. (Supplied by Norrie Price)

Hand of friendship: Alan Gilzean shakes hands with Benthaus as the Dundee team applaud the Germans into the dressing room (DC Thomson)

Tall Ships Go: Thousands turned out to watch the Unicorn *gracefully move down river to make way for the building of the Tay Road Bridge (DC Thomson)*

The man holding the quill: Former Dundee player turned Courier *journalist Tommy Gallacher (pictured with his son Mark) covered every match during the European Cup run. (DC Thomson)*

Duty Free: The Dundee squad pictured at London Airport on the return journey following the first leg defeat against Sporting Lisbon in Portugal. (DC Thomson)

Come rain or shine: The Sporting players shrugged off the weather to go sightseeing and shopping for gifts before the match. (DC Thomson)

The Lions of Lisbon: The Sporting players are put through their paces at Dens Park ahead of the following night's return leg. (DC Thomson)

Hat-trick hero: Alan Gilzean was too hot to handle for the Portuguese side of Lisbon and scored his second consecutive treble in European home games (DC Thomson)

Touch of class: Wing king Hugh Robertson pulls a high ball down from the air during a fine Dens display against Sporting. (DC Thomson)

The Big Freeze: The Dens groundsmen clear the snow from the pitch in January 1963 during what was one of the worst winters on record. (DC Thomson)

Man in a Suitcase: The bespectacled Anderlecht legend Joseph Jurion proves a crowd favourite as he leaves Tay Bridge Station on arrival in Dundee. (DC Thomson)

Top Marks: Congratulations all round as lecturer and part-time hero Alan Cousin scores the first for Dundee as the Dark Blues defeat Anderlecht to reach the semi-final. (DC Thomson)

Up Wi' the Bonnets: These Dundee fans get ready to leave Dickson Travel and head off on the long journey to the San Siro in April 1963. (DC Thomson)

Don't Dream It's Over: Dundee stand-in captain Bobby Seith and Milan skipper Cesare Maldini join together for the coin toss before the return leg. (DC Thomson)

Under Pressure: Milan goalkeeper Ghezzi stands firm as Dundee go all-out to get the early goals that might have given them a chance at Dens. (DC Thomson)

Heading for glory: Dundee striker Alan Gilzean and Milan captain Cesare Maldini go up for a high ball during another home attack in the second leg. (DC Thomson)

End of the affair: There was to be no fairy-tale ending for Dundee against Milan but the European Cup run will live long in the memory. (DC Thomson)

A new beginning: The new Tay Road Bridge is pictured under construction in 1963 which ultimately changed the city's landscape forever. (DC Thomson)

The salty dog was hoping to visit the *Unicorn*, now moved from her berth of 89 years at the Earl Grey Dock to make way for the Tay Road Bridge.

The Sporting players rested in their rooms in the afternoon before they paid their first visit to Dens Park, where 32,000 tickets had already been sold for the match.

There was growing excitement among the Dundee fans, who were relishing another big European night. Only ground tickets remained available before kick-off.

Sporting arrived at Dens to train at 5.30pm. Juca kept them inside the dressing room for 40 minutes to go over Sunday's domestic defeat.

The squad finally emerged in their green tracksuits with white flashes to be put through their paces on a bitterly windy evening following the heavy rain. Centre-half Lúcio was taking no chances with the cold and wore a woolly sweater under his tracksuit top and a pair of white stockings over his hands. Juca joined the fashion show by wearing a white jockey cap while conducting the 90-minute session with his whistle in his mouth.

The Sporting players reserved high praise afterwards for the Dens pitch, which they had expected to be muddy after all the rain. The surface was perfect. The Portuguese players were also impressed by the floodlights.

Goalkeeper Carvalho, who had a bruised shin, and midfielder Júlio, who was suffering a slight knee strain, stayed behind to receive treatment from Lawrie Smith. They received attention at the request of the Sporting Club doctor, one of four medics attached to the club, who could also call upon a surgeon and heart specialist.

Dundee would be giving winger Hugh Robertson until the last possible minute to prove his fitness after he missed the last two games because of his ankle injury.

Time was just as big an issue for the Norwegian match officials. They didn't have a clue when the match started!

The bewildered Norwegians arrived at Tay Bridge Station on Tuesday night at 7pm after travelling from Glasgow following their flight from Oslo via Copenhagen.

Referee Erling-Rolf Olsen and his two linesmen, Bjørn Borgersen and Mr K. Bruun, got a taxi to the Royal British Hotel on arrival in the city. The only orders they had been given were when to arrive in Dundee and which hotel to book into. Olsen said that nobody had told them when the match was scheduled to start the following evening.

'We went into the lounge and asked anyone if they knew what time the match started,' he said. 'One person told us half-past six and the next one we asked said half-past seven!'

They waited until they got the following day's copy of *The Courier* and looked in the sports pages to find the kick-off time.

The second leg would be the first match Olsen had taken charge of in the European Cup. There was a pool of seven international-class referees from Norway and this was the first time any of the officials had been in Scotland.

Olsen was a former player himself, having turned out for the Oslo-based club Skeid, which once played a friendly against Queen's Park.

'In Norway we have three leagues,' he said. 'I have been refereeing for 16 years and have handled four international games. The last one was the Sweden–Finland game in Helsinki in June. I find it rather cold here but it's much the same as in our country.'

The officials went window shopping in Dundee on Wednesday morning. Borgersen was sporting a bright tartan scarf, which he bought in Sweden to look the part in Scotland. Afterwards they went to the Dundee FC secretary's office in Reform Street to collect their tickets to get in.

Dundee's opponents also played the role of tourists on the morning of the match when they went on a bus tour of the city, followed by a rest in the afternoon. The Portuguese party had been invited to the City Chambers to meet Lord Provost McManus but had to turn him down because of prior engagements.

Dundee were still sweating over the fitness of Robertson and there was some good news when he emerged during the morning training session. He was kicking a ball and being given the chance to prove he could start. Shankly wanted him to be 100% fit and insisted he was not prepared to field him if there was any risk of him breaking down again against Sporting.

Doug Houston was waiting in the wings to replace Robertson, although Shankly stressed he would be leaving the decision to the last possible minute.

The Sporting players arrived two hours before kick-off to limber up on what was being described as 'the most thrilling midweek programme in Scottish sport for years'. Dunfermline against Everton in the Inter-

Cities Fairs Cup and Tottenham versus Rangers in the European Cup Winners' Cup were also taking place on the same evening.

Spurs manager Bill Nicholson might have slightly overcooked the pudding when he dubbed that evening's Rangers tie 'the greatest game on Earth', although the pairing of the two British sides in the Cup Winners' Cup had overshadowed the draw for the European Cup when both draws were made at the same meeting in Berne. The British press certainly awaited the Battle of Britain with eager anticipation.

Dundee supporters were backing Spurs on the night because former Dens Park goalkeeper Bill Brown was between the sticks for the White Hart Lane outfit. Brown was one of Dundee's all-time greats and he had also played in the World Cup finals in Sweden for Scotland.

Brown eventually left Dens to be replaced by an equally imposing structure. When Dundee sold him to Tottenham in 1959, his £16,500 transfer fee helped to pay for new floodlights and a covered enclosure a year later!

Highlights of all three European games were being shown on both the BBC and STV. *Sports Special* from 10.15pm on the BBC would feature one hour of highlights, with STV's *Scotsport* giving a 30-minute slot to the matches.

The gates at Dens Park opened at 6pm ahead of the 7.30pm kick-off with six cash turnstiles operating for the sale of unsold tickets.

Hundreds of cars converged on the ground but there were few hold-ups with 22 police officers on traffic duty. The efforts of the boys in blue were helped somewhat by many of the drivers who parked their cars in fringe areas rather than try to find a spot outside Dens Park. The nearby Fleming Gardens didn't have a free parking space in the entire housing scheme, with vehicles parked in unbroken lines on both sides of the road.

The Pipes and Drums of The Black Watch played from 6.45pm before the teams came out. Sporting were desperate to book their place in the next round. Their rivals Benfica were favourites to book a place in the quarter-finals following a 1-1 draw in the away leg of their second-round, first-leg tie against Norrkoping from Sweden.

Nuno Braz became the centre of attention as he tucked himself in at the end of the press box with his microphone. He was there to give a running commentary to his countrymen with the match being transmitted direct to Portugal, France, Spain, Africa and Brazil, but he was sticking out like a sore thumb thanks to a shopkeeper with Dundee United leanings who had clearly pulled a fast one on the poor commentator. Braz was the only person at Dens wearing a Dundee United scarf!

'I bought it this morning to keep the cold out,' he said.

The big game was also being broadcast live on the Toc H radio service which provided football commentary to the local hospitals in Dundee.

Around 32,000 fans were inside Dens Park. The centre of the town was practically deserted, including the pubs which were usually thronged all evening.

Former Aberdeen player Lachie McMillan was among those in the crowd willing the home side to overturn the deficit.

He got the train to Dundee after flying into London from Lisbon.

'They'll have to go some to beat Sporting,' he said. 'This is a first-class side. I think their narrow lead will be enough for them but I hope I'm wrong.'

Dundee: Slater, Hamilton, Cox, Seith, Ure, Wishart, Smith, Penman, Cousin, Gilzean, Robertson.

Sporting: Carvalho, Lino, Hilário, Carlos, Lúcio, Júlio, Figueiredo, Osvaldo, Mascarenhas, Geo, Morais.

Dundee proved they were a team that should not be written off.

Victory was never in doubt from the first minute and, although Alan Gilzean was the hat-trick hero in a 4-1 win, it was 38-year-old Gordon Smith who ran the show.

He was the real architect of the victory and had a hand in three of the four goals.

Dundee threw everything into attack from kick-off to get an early goal. Only the offside flag stopped encouraging moves in the opening exchanges.

Dundee broke the deadlock on 13 minutes when Smith beat two men before sending a perfect ball through to Gilzean. Gilzean ran on to beat Carvalho with a low drive from 15 yards.

Dundee's passing was sloppy despite taking the lead. Sporting almost pulled level on 17 minutes but Mascarenhas struck a wild shot over the bar.

Gilzean then troubled Sporting again with a 25-yard attempt, followed up with another strong effort which hit the side netting.

Sporting switched wingers in a bid to wrong-foot the Dundee defence. The wingers had just switched flanks when Dundee almost went two-up in 35 minutes after Smith shot on the turn following a slip from Alan Cousin.

Sporting could have gone ahead on aggregate just three minutes later but goalkeeper Bert Slater threw himself full-length to touch a pile-driver from Geo behind for a corner.

Crucially, Dundee scored again on the stroke of half-time when Cousin jumped highest in the box to head home off the underside of the crossbar from Smith's cross.

The break didn't stop Dundee's momentum and they came out of the traps flying. Cousin almost increased Dundee's advantage but his shot flew over from 18 yards.

Dundee were now totally in control and creating chance after chance, but Sporting were still dangerous on the counter-attack. They created an opening but Figueiredo struck straight at Slater before Dundee went three-up on 53 minutes following some more Smith magic on the wing. He managed to pick out Gilzean with the perfect pass and Dundee's top scorer ran 25 yards before letting fly with a drive from the edge of the box which beat Carvalho.

On 59 minutes Gilzean got his hat-trick, his second in the competition. Smith and Bobby Seith worked the ball out to Andy Penman on the right wing. Penman put in a low cross which was clinically poked home by Gilzean from close range.

Sporting fought back desperately and managed to reduce the deficit six minutes later to give themselves some hope of turning the tide. A pass from Mascarenhas cut through the Dundee defence. The ball found Figueiredo completely unmarked and he beat Slater at his far post.

On 71 minutes Gilzean missed a gilt-edged chance to restore Dundee's four-goal advantage on the night. He took too long in front of goal from a Seith pass and Dundee were eventually pulled up by the offside flag.

Gilzean was proving too hot to handle and two minutes later Carvalho managed to punch clear what looked like a certain goal for the Coupar Angus man.

Sporting almost got another goal with six minutes left to make things nervy but Slater got to the ball first as Mascarenhas lined up a shot from inside the six-yard box.

Dundee held on for a 4-1 win.

They would now take their place in the last eight of the European Cup alongside AC Milan, Dukla Prague, Benfica, Feyenoord, Stade de Reims, Galatasaray and Anderlecht.

The atmosphere was incredible. The huge crowd meant chaotic traffic scenes, in some places taking ten minutes to drive a few hundred yards. The situation was exacerbated by thousands of spectators walking along the road after pouring out of the ground in celebration.

There were mixed fortunes for the two other Scottish clubs in European action.

Jock Stein's Dunfermline scored a remarkable 2-0 victory against 'Bank of England' side Everton at East End Park for a 2-1 aggregate win in the Inter-Cities Fairs Cup.

In the night's other 'Battle of Britain', thousands of Rangers supporters flocked to White Hart Lane only to see their side ripped apart 5-2 by a rampant

Tottenham in the first leg of their European Cup Winners' Cup clash.

Dundee put on an after-match banquet for Sporting in the Queen's Hotel where presents were exchanged between the clubs. The directors of Sporting were each presented with a Dundee tie by chairman James Gellatly, who was just back from a lengthy business trip to America. Each player received a tartan tie comprising four different tartans and Mr Gellatly gave Sporting a solid silver salver with an inscription to commemorate the game.

Sporting president Commodore Pascoal returned the compliment in true seafaring fashion with a delightful donation of a filigree silver model of an ancient Portuguese galleon. It remains in the Dens Park boardroom to this day, but Bobby Wishart said that gifts given after games weren't always so impressive.

The former Dons player recalled an Aberdeen versus Chelsea challenge match in 1955 after the sides had won their respective championships. Wishart netted a fine goal as Aberdeen ran out 4-3 winners. It was billed an unofficial British Championship decider by an excited media. Afterwards both sides were presented with tartan travelling rugs as a memento.

Commodore Pascoal predicted there would be more glory days to come for Wishart, the man now starring for Dundee at left-half. He said that he was disappointed that his side had been beaten but admitted that the better team won.

In any case, he felt that victory itself wasn't all-important. He said the idea behind the European Cup competition was to create good friendship and this had been clearly established between the two clubs.

'Dundee will win the cup,' he said. 'Nothing else can happen as long as they have Smith. I told Hilário, my powerful left-back, who once got the better of the great Garrincha, to cover Smith. But Hilário failed, as all the others soon will against this football veteran.'

Commodore Pascoal, who was drinking his fifth consolation whisky, also said he was surprised Dundee did not draw a capacity crowd for the second-leg match. He said, 'Dundee deserve to play before at least 30,000 fans every time. I am surprised they have gates lower than half that figure. With a big support I think they could achieve great things in football.'

Dundee's winning run to the league title the previous season had lifted the crowds from a 12,000 average up to around 17,000. Despite being league champions, Dundee's gates had not markedly improved, though the league form had been disappointing. The two European ties at Dens had pulled in crowds of 25,000 and 32,000. In contrast, the post-war boom had seen bumper gates all around. And when star attraction Billy Steel had led the line in the 1950s, Dundee consistently averaged over 20,000 per home game, on several occasions pulling in well over 30,000.

Sporting midfielder David Júlio accepted that the better team won and, as in the first leg, identified the 'Smith factor' as being decisive. 'Dundee's forwards were far more dangerous than us,' he said. 'Gordon Smith is a great player.'

Dundee right-back Alex Hamilton also praised Smith's influence after the match. 'He encouraged me to overlap, and, along with Bobby Seith, we made a formidable right-wing trio,' he said. 'When I came up, Smith would play back to Seith before moving inside to create space for me on the outside. We played some great triangular stuff and time and again Bobby would open things up with a lob out to the wing.'

The Sporting team spoke of their high regard for the whole Dundee team but, as well as wing wizard Smith, they reserved special praise for Ian Ure.

The Portuguese press raved about Ure's performance over the two games, with one journalist describing him as the greatest centre-half he'd ever seen and 'a player who would be welcomed into any of the world's greatest sides'.

The referee and linesmen from Norway were also in attendance at the banquet and were given a Sporting Club pennant and Dundee ties.

'It was fair play from both teams – no trouble,' said referee Erling-Rolf Olsen. 'I thought the crowd's singing and chanting was wonderful.'

He also said the playing surface was one of the best he had seen despite the fact he had officiated in Italy and Greece and various other countries in Europe.

Hero of the hour Smith was in no doubt that Dundee could go all the way to Wembley. He said, 'Dundee can win the European Cup. After beating teams of the calibre of Cologne and Sporting I see no reason why Dundee need be afraid of any team in the competition.'

Smith had already made it clear to his team-mates that becoming the first British team to lift the European Cup was not an impossible feat. The veteran, of course, had already proved himself a success in the soothsaying stakes after correctly predicting Dundee would win the league in 1961/62.

The banquet finally broke up just after 12.15am. The Portuguese party had an early start and were due to leave Dundee at 7.30am by bus for Turnhouse before flying to Lisbon via London.

Just days later the Civil Aviation Licensing Authority finally granted Dundee's airstrip at Riverside Park official status. The 1,100-yard strip had so far only been available for charter planes under 6,000 tonnes but the granting of the licence meant scheduled services could now be laid on. Lord Provost McManus announced that another 400 yards could be added to the runway almost immediately, which would facilitate the possibility of bringing in bigger aircraft.

Meanwhile, in the wider world, the Soviet Union suggested there might be more touching down than just planes in future when they affirmed there was life on Mars.

An article in the Soviet Communist party newspaper *Pravda* carried front page reports of the 'success' of a mission being carried out by Russia's spacecraft *Mars I*.

Dundee's own quest for world domination – albeit on a European, rather than global scale – was now grounded for the time being.

The Dark Blues would not know their next opponents for several weeks, with the draw for the quarter-final not due to take place in Berne until December. Furthermore, the winter shutdown across most of the continent – none in the UK back then – meant Dundee could forget about the European Cup until February when the quarter-finals were due.

But things don't always go to plan. Britain was set for its worst weather in over 200 years.

Chapter 8

The Big Freeze

'We all feel like big-game hunters with no gun and no bullets.'

Dundee defender Ian Ure

NOW INTO November, Dundee were brought back to earth from their European heroics as Sean Connery prepared to save the world as secret agent James Bond.

A 2-1 home win against Airdrie was followed by single-goal defeats in Glasgow to Partick Thistle and Third Lanark either side of a scoreless stalemate at snow-covered Dens against Celtic.

Dundee's title challenge was shaken and stirred as the first Bond movie, adapted from Ian Fleming's books, was being shown at the Gaumont in the Cowgate. A month earlier, *Dr No* had been released to a selected 100 cinemas throughout the country. Now it was going out to the public at large.

As it was, 007's creator had strong Dundee connections. Ian Fleming's grandfather, Robert Fleming, was born in Lochee and rose from his position in the clerk's office of a local textile firm to become an international financier who profitably invested in the booming American railway industry.

Robert Fleming became a hugely wealthy man and was one of Dundee's most remarkable success stories. He made many generous bequests to the city and its new University College, while the Fleming Gardens Estate near Dens Park was erected as a result of his gift of £155,000 to improve housing for workers.

It was not only the Bond films that took the world by storm. Talented composer John Barry was also to spring to prominence. Though initially uncredited for his work on the film, Barry, who was a successful band leader with the John Barry Seven, gained ever-increasing recognition when the 'James Bond Theme' peaked at number 13 in the UK singles chart. The John Barry Seven was subsequently booked to appear at Dundee's Top Ten Club at the Palais near the end of the year.

Not to be outdone, Alan Gilzean again hit the headlines, netting seven in a 10-2 mauling of luckless Queen of the South at Dens Park in December. Gillie's seven goals equalled the club record for a single game, set by Albert Juliussen 15 years earlier.

There were mitigating circumstances. Queens goalkeeper George Farm had collided with Gilzean before Dundee's second goal and was stretchered off after just 12 minutes. Later, the predatory Gilzean went to visit the stricken keeper at Dundee Royal Infirmary and declared himself embarrassed at matching Juliussen's record in such circumstances.

For his part, the popular 'Julie', part of the Dundee side which won back-to-back Scottish League B Division championships, got his seven goals in a 10-0 win against Dunfermline at Dens in March 1947. The six-goal record he overtook hadn't lasted long – Juliussen himself set it at Alloa in an identical scoreline the week before! Rapid scoring was nothing new for the strapping Juliussen, who had previously scored seven in the first half for Dundee against a British Army Select. To even things up, he swapped sides for the second half, though in only managing a modest six for the opposition, he was unable to retrieve the deficit.

The Dark Blues were now on a more consistent run with victories away to St Mirren and Raith Rovers either side of a 2-2 draw with Motherwell. Dundee would need to raise their game to a different level if they were to get past RSC Anderlecht after being paired with the Belgian champions in the quarter-final draw.

Anderlecht, or to give them their full name, Royal Sporting Club Anderlechtois, had seen off the mighty Real Madrid in the preliminary round before defeating CSKA Sofia of Bulgaria 4-2 on aggregate.

The Belgian club was making its mark following a severe setback in the early days of the European Cup, when they suffered a 10-0 defeat by Manchester United in 1956. Now they were the best-supported club in Belgium, with crowds averaging over 20,000 at the Astrid Park stadium in Brussels. They included nine internationals in their ranks, with Paul Van Himst and Joseph Jurion regarded amongst the cream of European footballers.

The hugely talented Van Himst, who averaged a goal in every second game, made his Anderlecht debut at 16 and within a year was playing for Belgium. He was still only 19 but had been voted Belgium's footballer of the year twice, with Barcelona and Real Madrid among the clubs now linked with signing him.

The brilliant Jurion, who scored the winning goal against Real Madrid, suffered from myopia and wore glasses on the pitch, making him instantly recognisable. He had worn specs from the age of seven and used to remove them to play football. As his sight deteriorated, Jurion was persuaded to try contact lenses, which he didn't take to. But his career was saved when a Brussels optician designed special glasses for him with unbreakable lenses, soft metal frames and leather straps. The contraption resembled a pilot's helmet. He would be travelling to Dundee with three pairs in his luggage, as he always did when going abroad.

The first leg would take place in Belgium where inside-left Alan Gilzean received a letter from the Poperinge branch of the Dundee Supporters' Club. Poperinge was 80 miles from Brussels and eight-year-old Ronald Sutherland was the sole member of the fledgling club!

Ronald – born in Belgium to Scottish parents – said he had been telling his schoolmates just what the Dens Parkers were going to do to Anderlecht. He also predicted Gilzean would score twice.

'I don't know if I'll see Ronald when we go to Brussels,' said Gilzean. 'But I'll certainly make a point of sending him an autographed picture of the team.'

The European Cup draw and the pairing with Anderlecht re-ignited excitement amongst Dundee supporters back home. Also of great interest to them now were the other ties which made up the last eight: Galatasaray against AC Milan, Stade de Reims against Feyenoord and Benfica against Dukla Prague.

It would be fair to say that the knowledge of European geography among school pupils in Dundee had come on leaps and bounds in the past few months.

The approach of the festive season brought the much-acclaimed *Lawrence of Arabia* to the nation's cinema screens while a starring role in two consecutive first-team games in December prompted defender George Ryden to knock on Shankly's door and withdraw his transfer request.

'I asked Mr Shankly to forget I ever mentioned the matter,' he said. 'Now that I know I've got a chance of playing in the big team I'm happy. When I asked away I hadn't played one first-team game since signing in 1958 and I figured I'd never be promoted from the reserves. Now I'm quite satisfied knowing

I'm being considered for the big team when a vacancy crops up.'

Ryden was Ian Ure's deputy at centre-half. Both shared the same digs in Dundee and were spotted by scout Jimmy Ross.

'Ian and I are the best of pals but I haven't tried to imitate his style,' said Ryden. 'Like him, however, I put everything I've got into the game.'

Ryden played at right-half when he was promoted by Shankly. Switching positions was nothing new to Ryden, who started life as an inside-right. Two of his brothers also went on to play at senior level; John with Alloa and Spurs, Hugh with Bristol Rovers.

Ryden signed for Dundee despite offers from Chelsea and Leeds and most of his spare time was taken up with the Top Ten Club in Dundee. Ryden was on the four-man organising committee and helped bring some of the biggest pop stars to Dundee. The likes of David Bowie and the Bee Gees would appear there.

But not all was to be good cheer. This period heralded the advent of a prolonged freeze which was not to relent until March 1963.

Fog and ice had already caused chaos when snow began falling on 24 December to give Glasgow its first white Christmas since 1938. Initially it was welcomed, particularly by children who saw it as a bit of holiday fun, but soon the mood turned to despair.

On Boxing Day, the 1.30pm Glasgow to London express, continuing on through frozen points and warning signals in heavy snow, ploughed into the back of a stationary train near Crewe. The rear carriages of the train to Birmingham were crushed and 18 people lost their lives, with another 30 badly injured.

As far as football was concerned, the situation was the worst in living memory and broke all records for the postponement of matches. Throughout January, February and the early days of March, the weather continued to play havoc.

Dundee's game against Aberdeen at Pittodrie on New Year's Day surprisingly received the go-ahead from the referee despite the snow-covered surface. It was a must-win match with Shankly's side already nine points behind league leaders Rangers with Partick Thistle, Kilmarnock, Aberdeen and Celtic close behind.

In the event, the Dark Blues went down to a 1-0 defeat. When they suffered a further reverse, 3-2 to Clyde at a muddy Shawfield four days later, any lingering hopes of a championship challenge disappeared.

'I'm beginning to realise just what Rangers have to stand up to every week,' said Dens boss Shankly. 'League champions are there to be shot at. Everybody's out to beat them. So, as present champions, we have to keep right on the top line – all the time.'

The Dens Parkers did, however, progress to the second round of the Scottish Cup with a 5-1 win the following Saturday at Inverness Caley before the football programme was totally wiped out.

Various ideas were tried to beat the freeze, notably across the road at Tannadice.

Manager Jerry Kerr and the Dundee United board moved heaven and earth to try to make the pitch playable for their Scottish Cup tie against Albion Rovers which was scheduled for 26 January.

Fire braziers were tried before William Briggs and Sons, roadmakers at the Camperdown Refinery at Dundee docks, brought in a tar burner to melt the Tannadice ice sheet. It also burned off all the grass. Several lorryloads of sand were then spread over the pitch.

Legend has it that this was the time when United supporters became known as the Arabs since the pitch increasingly appeared like a desert wasteland. What isn't in doubt was just how bad the weather was in the early months of 1963.

Entire houses were buried under the snow as every part of the country was hit by the freak conditions. There was the solace of TV and radio, but in some areas communications were cut with phone lines down.

The Football Pools were an important part of the weekly routine for many but the ongoing postponement of games meant a succession of coupons we're declared void. By late January, however, they had a solution.

The newly formed Football Pools Panel initially comprised four famous ex-footballers – Ted Drake, Tom Finney, Tommy Lawton and George Young – along with former referee Arthur Ellis. They met behind closed doors to decide the theoretical results of matches and their predictions were broadcast on television. In total the panel determined the results on five Saturdays during the Big Freeze and were to become a regular feature in winters to come.

Meanwhile, ousted Dundee goalkeeper Pat Liney kept himself busy during the lay-off and got his chance in the spotlight again – as a singer at the JM Ballroom. He was booked to deliver a few ballads from 8.30pm to midnight on a night reserved for dancers in the 20 to 30 age group.

Liney was backed up by the orchestra and team-mates Alex Hamilton, on piano, and Hugh Robertson, on guitar or drums. Scotland right-back Hamilton was later to become the frontman of Hammy and the Hamsters, a group formed entirely of Dundee players who also performed locally.

Liney, though, was singing for his supper. He soon found himself back on the sidelines for Dundee's home game against Montrose in the second round of the Scottish Cup on 4 February. The tie went ahead on a snow-covered Dens Park but any worries over a possible upset disappeared as Dundee hit the Links Parkers with an avalanche of goals in a runaway 8-0 victory.

Elsewhere, things were deteriorating as major roads including the A9 and A90 were blocked during blizzard conditions. People in parts of Scotland were left stranded in trains. Some children were forced to remain overnight in snowbound schools.

For the first time in many years, ice was a navigational risk on the River Tay, with Broughty harbour beset by ice and the sea off the Ferry's 'Swanny Beach' looking like a scene from the Antarctic.

Nevertheless, construction of the Tay Road Bridge was due to commence on 29 March after Willie Logan was chosen as contractor. One of the influencing factors was his proposal to fabricate box girders for the bridge at the Caledon Shipyard.

Logan's firm almost lost out on winning the contract because of the Big Freeze as conditions prevented them driving from their northern base to Dundee. The deadline for tenders was 11am on 17 January. The problem was solved when they flew their recently purchased aircraft from Renfrew to Muir of Ord then down to the unmarked grass strip at Riverside in heavy snow. The documents were submitted at the City Chambers with 15 minutes to spare and were the last of the 16 tenders received.

Other parts of northern Europe had also been hit by the severe winter of 1962/63.

In anticipation of a bumper crowd for the European Cup tie with Dundee, Anderlecht had moved the game from Astrid Park to Heysel Stadium, the national stadium, also in Brussels. It could hold over 60,000 fans.

It was not only the venue that would change.

The first leg of the tie had been scheduled for 13 February in Brussels but freezing conditions dictated a postponement until 6 March. The news prompted Bob Brian of the *Scottish Daily Mail* to consider the Dark Blues' prospects.

He said, 'Next month will see Dundee established as one of Europe's top teams ... or just another Scottish club struggling to make ends meet with the hope that next season will be their year.

'The champions tag they won last season has had a mixed effect.

'It has given them the confidence to hold their own in the European Cup and it has made them the target for every name-seeking team in Scotland.

'The league form has been disappointing. The high tension of the European Cup has left them with a strong feeling of anti-climax on ordinary match days.

'Now they find themselves out of the title race. And although the Scottish and European Cups may be enough for any team to concentrate on, the tension is building.

'On March 6, Dundee go to Brussels for the first leg of their European tie with Anderlecht and on the following Wednesday Anderlecht are at Dens Park.

'This Saturday they meet Hibs in the Scottish Cup.

'These three games can make or break Dundee. Should they fail in both cup ties, their season will end there and then.

'The European Cup profits which have already been partly diminished by the lie-off, will disappear and Dundee will have achieved nothing except maybe earning a small reputation on the continent.

'But if they win both ties their reputation will soar. They will have a tidy sum in the bank and maybe, eventually a little silverware to put on display.

'Their league form has in no way dampened their confidence. Any Dundee player will tell you they can always pull out that little bit extra on the big occasion.

'Having seen them beat Cologne and Sporting Club, I am only too ready to agree.'

Meanwhile, the prolonged interruption to the football programme provided some time for measured debate. The future of the Scottish game had returned to the agenda as a result of the weather.

All 37 Scottish League clubs received a circular outlining a scheme for summer football which would go to a vote on 25 February. The proposal was that the season would run from March to the end of November with a break of two or three weeks in July. Scottish Cup ties would be brought in much earlier than usual at the beginning of May with the final at Hampden on a Saturday in June. The League Cup would be switched from the beginning of the season to nearer the end with the final in late November.

But with 34 league games, six League Cup sectional ties and one Scottish Cup tie, this meant a minimum of 41 games and would entail some two games per week over the projected 20-week season.

Ian Ure, meanwhile, had been handed the highly prestigious Scottish Footballer of the Year award for 1962, an honour richly deserved by the 23-year-old. He was a key figure in defence as Dundee lifted the title and proceeded to make their mark in the European Cup. Ure was a rising star and was to receive the same award as that first made to team-mate Gordon Smith, then at Hibs, back in 1951.

His performances had also been recognised by appearances for the Scotland international team as he battled with Celtic's captain Billy McNeill for the number five jersey. An Under-23 cap against England in March 1961 had been followed by a full Scotland appearance in the 2-0 win over Wales at Hampden in November that year.

That game had also marked a Scotland debut for Alex Hamilton and both, along with left-winger Hugh Robertson, had played in the World Cup play-off match against Czechoslovakia at what was to be their next European Cup stop, the Heysel Stadium in Brussels.

The Footballer of the Year presentation ceremony was held at Dundee's Caird Hall and manager Bob Shankly described the qualities the big defender brought to the side.

He highlighted him as a player who hated to lose and who was at his best when the chips were down and the battle hardest.

The fair-haired centre-half was the player opposition fans loved to hate, but behind the powerful physical presence was a man with a keen and discerning mind, and indeed was vice-chairman of the Scottish Professional Footballers' Association.

The lack of competitive games had left newspapers well short of material and in an interview with *The Courier*, Ure expressed his views on the future of Scottish football.

'I am 100% convinced that the clubs will vote against summer soccer when they meet on February 25,' he said. 'I agree with the view that it would not be a profitable switch and would put a heavier burden on the smaller clubs. But I say that the summer game would be very profitable in another direction – it would help greatly to bump up our playing standard.

'Winter football is the main drawback to Scotland's development as a football nation. Most foreign teams play the game on good grounds. We are asked to contend with snow, ice, rain, driving winds and mud.'

Dundee were now facing significant fixture congestion amid rising postponements and Ure called for an extension to the season.

He said, 'I know how the fans are feeling about football right now. You can take it from me that we players feel every bit as fed-up. Last Saturday I was like a lost soul. No games anywhere – it's absolute murder. We are existing in a world of clearing operations, inspections, another dose of frost which puts everybody back where they started. We all feel like big-game hunters with no gun and no bullets.'

News of Dundee FC's European Cup exploits had spread with Dutch magazine *Revue* the latest to have their say.

Describing the Dark Blues as 'the shock team of the competition', the article acknowledged that the

Dens Park side were capable of rising from levels of mediocrity to the heights of brilliance.

This, it went on, was well known in Scotland 'but for FC Cologne and Sporting Club Lisbon, it came as a tremendous shock.

'They must have left Dens numbed by the way they were reduced to also-rans by the scintillating Dundee.'

Back on the topic of reconstruction, league leaders Rangers spoke out against a change to summer football.

Manager Scot Symon said it would be 'quite wrong' to support 'any drastic change' and produced figures to show the clubs who supported the status quo had far bigger gates than those who were in favour of the proposed change. He need not have worried for, in a vote held in secret in Glasgow and lasting only an hour, 25 of the 37 Scottish League clubs voted against the charge.

It seemed that the freeze would never end.

On 26 February 1963, two Stanley men became the first people to walk across the frozen River Tay since 1898. Alec O'Brien and brother-in-law Ian Smith managed the feat at the picturesque Perthshire village of Burnmouth.

They abandoned an attempt to repeat the crossing on bicycles a few days later. 'It would be too risky,' said Alec. 'We were lucky to catch the right conditions on the first attempt.'

A Siamese cat decided to make a similar journey only to become marooned on a tiny island in Perth before returning home wet and hungry, but none the worse for her escapade.

The Belgian league programme had been paralysed for nine successive weeks and a three-inch covering of snow remained on the Heysel pitch at the beginning of March.

UEFA were even considering switching the European Cup Final at Wembley from 22 May to 1 June because of the ever-increasing fixture backlog.

But at long last came the much-needed thaw which allowed the snow to be cleared from the Heysel pitch, with a hot-air machine brought in to remove the remaining patches of ice.

Dundee had only played once in February against Montrose in the Scottish Cup and their chances of a competitive game before the first leg in Belgium were not looking good. The Scottish Cup tie against Hibernian and subsequent league game against

Dunfermline were called off because Dens Park remained unplayable.

Many of the ice patches on the Dens surface were thawing out in the sunshine but a spiking machine was having little effect on the solid ice area at the south end of the pitch.

Things got worse when a reserve match against Dunfermline at East End Park was also cancelled and Shankly admitted he was desperate for a competitive fixture.

'We must get a game somewhere, even if it is only against a junior team,' he said. 'The boys must get match practice and be relieved of the monotony of playing each other all the time.'

Alex Hamilton said weeks of strenuous games for the first team against the Dens reserves had been as difficult and frantic as any league match. He didn't agree Dundee would be underdogs because of a lack of competitive action and said they would be going to Brussels to win.

'Anderlecht are a mystery team to us,' he said. 'Nobody connected with the club has seen them in action. I don't think they can come any tougher than Cologne but Anderlecht will get our full respect. After all they went to Spain and held Real Madrid, then beat them in Brussels.

'There is a suggestion they may fox us with their offside tactics for which they are evidently notorious. I believe the Real attack was caught out 18 times. We'll have to deal with that if it happens but I am confident we have the players to beat their plans. Each one of our forwards has proved his ability to take the ball right through. So have the wing-halves and I must confess a liking for the attacking role.'

Hamilton described the Heysel Stadium as 'quite a showpiece'.

'We are told to expect a hard footing,' he said. 'That won't worry us because we have had to adapt ourselves to similar conditions during our training games. If by some chance there is a quick thaw and a heavy pitch, that, too, will not upset us. Most of us like heavy going.'

Hamilton said playing in the European Cup for Dundee was a dream come true.

'I never thought I'd be helping a team fight for the European Cup,' he said. 'Six years ago I was chapping at doors in West Lothian trying to sell insurance. Before then I had been stuck at an office desk then did most of my Army service in Germany.

'My ambitions have certainly been fulfilled in a real flood. In a season and a half I have had ten caps for Scotland, the league championship medal, and wonderful foreign travel. I've been to ten different countries and played against some of the finest left-wingers in the game. Football is the life when it works out like this.'

Wonderful foreign travel was indeed back on the horizon now the thaw had kicked in.

Brussels was up next, after a less-alluring trip to play East Fife at Methil.

Chapter 9

From Bayview to Brussels

*'This is one team I am praying we
shall not meet if we get to the final of
the European Cup.'*

AC Milan manager Nereo Rocco

DUNDEE HAD been offered the chance of a
competitive fixture in Ireland by both Drumcondra in
the Republic and Linfield in Belfast but they instead
opted to stay closer to home. A friendly was organised
against Second Division side East Fife at Bayview and
Shankly said he was pleased his team would leave for
Brussels with a game under their belt.

Anderlecht, too, were making their preparations
for the forthcoming European Cup quarter-final clash.
They arranged a friendly match against the French

team Valenciennes. In addition, the Belgian champions scheduled three days of special training in a small village just outside Brussels.

Back home, battle lines were drawn before Dundee's visit to Methil when it emerged their friendly would be in direct competition with a match between Raith Rovers and Dundee United at Starks Park. Raith were concerned about the impact this would have on gate receipts and eventually the East Fife versus Dundee kick-off was moved to noon to avoid a 3pm clash.

It was also agreed that the Methil match would take place behind closed doors. The match didn't turn out to be private though, with a single door remaining open which allowed for a steady stream of spectators to trickle through to watch.

Dundee fielded their strongest team with the exception of veteran playmaker Gordon Smith, who was given a rest and replaced in the starting line-up by Bobby Waddell.

East Fife played some good football and went 2-0 up at half-time. Second half goals from Waddell, Bobby Wishart and a brace from Andy Penman gave ring-rusty Dundee a 4-2 victory. Dundee's greater urgency after the break came from manager Shankly stressing at half-time that anything but a convincing win would provide a psychological boost to Anderlecht.

The fact it took Dundee so long to score was mainly down to East Fife centre-half Jake Young, who wanted to prove himself against his former employers. The ex-Dens Parker had a great game at the back. He saved three certain goals with his defending as Dundee upped the ante in the second half.

East Fife manager Charlie McCaig said, 'I was pleased with our showing but don't let us kid ourselves, Dundee were playing well within themselves.'

For his part, Shankly was unstinting in his praise of his opponents after the game. 'We can't thank Charlie McCaig and his directors enough for providing us with the opportunity of a game before meeting Anderlecht,' he said. 'We appreciated it all the more because of the fuss that it created. It says a lot for them that they were still prepared to play, even behind closed doors, and to get no gate money in return. And on top of that the hospitality they have given us since our arrival here, has been, to say the least, first class.'

Seven of Anderlecht's international players were in the Belgium team which defeated Holland 1-0 in Rotterdam on 2 March. Joseph Jurion suffered a slight injury during training and wasn't risked in the Sunday international which was played on a very poor pitch. Laurent Verbiest and Paul Van Himst received knocks during the match but would be fit for the Dundee game.

The imposing Verbiest was a cultured defender who joined Anderlecht from KV Oostende in 1960. He was nicknamed 'Lorenzo le Magnifique' and had been likened to AC Milan's Cesare Maldini, a man of similar physique and an outstanding footballer.

The highly respected *Sunday Times* football correspondent Brian Glanville acknowledged the Belgian's influence but commented, 'Verbiest can appear nonchalant and self-pleasing and sometimes leaves little margin for error. It will be intriguing to contrast him with Dundee's Ian Ure when the sides meet.'

Back in Scotland, snowdrifts and ice were shrinking fast. Burns in the Dundee area were running high. The Dighty burst its banks at several places, flooding fields and back gardens.

Dundee skipper Bobby Cox also found himself in deep trouble the next morning. He was almost left on the platform following a last-minute rush to Tay Bridge Station where a party of 14 players and officials were leaving by train for Edinburgh on Monday. Cox found himself with little time to spare so he asked his garage mechanic to drive him to the station, where he was greeted by jeers as the last to arrive.

George Ryden and Bobby Waddell were added to the travelling squad at the expense of Doug Houston and Alex Stuart. A large crowd including Dundee director Jack Swadel turned up at the station to give them a send-off. Directors James Gellatly and Robert Crichton, manager Shankly, trainer Sammy Kean and physio Lawrie Smith were among the party which left Dundee.

Smith, Slater, Wishart, Cousin and Brown joined the party at Edinburgh where they were taken by coach straight to the airport from Waverley Station.

Dundee eventually flew out from Turnhouse at 3.40pm following a 20-minute delay. Planes had earlier been diverted to Renfrew because of early morning fog which lifted as the day went on. The logjam which pushed back take-off ensured a subsequent rush to change planes at London. They left the capital on a jet and still managed to arrive half an hour ahead of schedule in Brussels at 7.25pm despite the travel delays.

The Dundee party were greeted on arrival by four Anderlecht officials and a string of Belgian photographers and journalists. They would be staying at the plush Palace Hotel and the first thing they noticed on touching down in Brussels was the improvement in the weather. The temperature had risen significantly since Saturday and Brussels was nowhere near as cold as was being experienced back home in Scotland.

The weather and the decision by Anderlecht to impose a domestic TV blackout on the quarter-final match prompted ticket sales to rocket. Anderlecht officials had initially agreed for the game to be televised to six countries on the Eurovision link provided it was not made known in advance. A national newspaper, which had been given the rights to televise the match, then announced they were planning to show it domestically. That action prompted Anderlecht to pull the rug from under them.

Dundee were now expected to play before a near-capacity crowd of 60,000 fans. Not all of them, however, would be Anderlecht supporters in a city which was sharply divided between Flemish and French speaking Belgians. Dundee were told on arrival that they could expect considerable support from the French-speaking element of the city.

The Belgian journalists at the airport who gathered to meet Dundee off the plane said Heysel Stadium was in perfect condition and quite soft on top. Dundee planned a couple of training sessions for the following day but were told they would not be allowed to train at the Heysel ahead of the match.

Anderlecht general secretary Eugène Steppé said that was out of the question, but they were willing to let Dundee train at Astrid Park on Tuesday. Steppé, along with French journalist Gabriel Hanot, was one of the pioneers in formulating the idea for the European Cup and had been present at the official launch of the competition in 1955.

Anderlecht were resting at their village headquarters. Joseph Jurion and Paul Van Himst were both declared fit following the weekend international match.

The Dark Blues arrived at the Palace Hotel to be greeted by a fleet of 20 new cars with Dundee FC placards fixed on their roofs which had been put at their disposal.

Back in Dundee, one gentleman was particularly well dressed, all decked out in a Dundee club blazer, tie and scarf, ready to board a bus in the city's Reform Street. He was among the 40 Dundee fans who were travelling to Brussels on a Dickson's coach which left the travel firm's office at 6pm on Monday night.

Sydney Hood, from Fintry Road, was taking his nine-year-old son Ramsay to Brussels for the match and decided to look the part, despite being a Dundee United supporter himself! Young Ramsay, whose great favourite was Ian Ure, posed on the bus steps with eight-year-old Kenneth Clark and held aloft their blue and white banner which read: 'Dundee Champions 1961-1962. Up Wi' The Bonnets.'

Now it was the turn of Anderlecht to change their tune. Dundee turned up for training at Astrid Park on Tuesday morning only to be told they couldn't play on the pitch. Anderlecht officials said they didn't want the pitch cut up because they wanted to preserve it ahead of the team's league match against Ghent on Sunday.

Dundee were instead offered the use of one of Anderlecht's two practice grounds inside the Astrid Stadium, but Shankly turned down the invitation. Both were mud heaps, frozen and rutted on top, and Shankly didn't want to risk any of his players.

In the end, Dundee had to make do with an hour's training on four tennis courts. Parts of the clay courts still had a coating of ice when training started before the frost melted and the surface became transformed into a blood-red quagmire.

Scaffold goalposts were rigged up and Sammy Kean finished off the session by organising a seven-a-side game which took place within a confined area of roughly 60 yards by 40 yards.

Dundee were not alone. Apart from their travelling supporters, representatives of another of the city's institutions were in attendance in Brussels. Stewart's Cream of the Barley (Dundee) whisky company, founded in 1825 and then based in Castle Street, had advertised in the club programme since the late 1940s. Now they were expanding their business throughout Europe and beyond and took the opportunity to visit Brussels and mix business with pleasure. A post-training photo opportunity was arranged with the Dundee squad and the players each provided with a bottle of Scotland's finest!

Shankly approached Steppé again at the end of the session to see if there were any other suitable pitches in the area. He contacted 20 clubs but either the grounds had been used on Sunday and were badly cut up or they were required for the following Sunday and couldn't be played on.

The players then relaxed in the afternoon. Some of them went shopping before Dundee trained again on the courts on Tuesday night. Afterwards they went to have their first look at the Heysel Stadium.

Shankly also arranged for a final session at the tennis courts the morning before the match, but it was already game, set and match according to the Belgian media.

The general opinion in the sports pages was that Anderlecht would establish a big enough lead in the first leg to take to Dundee for the return match a week later. The media were also guilty of whipping up ill-feeling against Alan Gilzean in the build-up with a case of mistaken identity.

Gilzean was wrongly singled out as the man who injured the Cologne goalkeeper Fritz Ewert at Dens when it was actually Alan Cousin who was involved in the accidental clash. They also brought up the fact that Gillie had been involved in a collision with Queen of the South's George Farm as further proof that he 'makes it tough for goalkeepers'.

'I'm getting used to it now,' he said. 'After all, they said it in Cologne and they said it again in Lisbon. I wish someone would let them know that when I go for a ball in the air I'm just as liable to be injured as anyone else.'

Gilzean said Dundee had a healthy respect for Anderlecht, knowing they would have to contend with a team that had beaten Real Madrid in the same stadium.

Meanwhile, the TV blackout put in place by Anderlecht officials was lifted just before the game, although the match still wouldn't be shown live in Belgium. Anderlecht agreed that it could be broadcast on the Eurovision link in Scotland, England, Denmark, Holland, Germany, Italy and Switzerland. Celtic's cup replay against Hearts on the same night ruled out the chance of fans in Scotland seeing it live but highlights were to be shown on the BBC and STV.

There might have been a TV blackout in Belgium but Dundee did get a prime-time spot on Belgian TV thanks to a city barmaid. Millie Waterston, known to Dundee players and fans at the Royal British Hotel, appeared in a television feature which previewed the first-leg match.

Mrs Waterston was interviewed by a TV crew who had been struck by her faith in the team when they stayed at the hotel during the match between Dundee and Cologne. They decided to interview her when they returned to Scotland to film Dundee players and the footage included a shot of Mrs Waterston with her fingers crossed.

When Mrs Waterston, whose brothers and sisters were also lifelong Dundee supporters, made the gesture for the Belgian interviewer, he was puzzled, asking what it meant. 'I told Ricky [the interviewer] that keeping your fingers crossed meant you were wishing for something to come true,' she said. 'I was wishing for Dundee to win at Anderlecht.'

Mrs Waterston, whose mother was also a great Dundee fan, said her daughter had also been brought up 'in the faith'. Leaning over the bar where she was serving, she told the TV cameras she was sure Dundee would leave Belgium with a victory.

Also enjoying star billing the night before Dundee's match was wrestling hero George Kidd, who faced England's Alan Dennison at the Caird Hall. The venue had a rich history of wrestling dating back to legendary heavyweight Bert Assirati topping the bill before and after the Second World War.

Kidd began wrestling when he enlisted in the Royal Navy in 1943. After the war he went to England to pursue his passion and began a glorious career. The city's wrestling idol was cheered on to victory against Dennison while the Dundee players were grappling with the heat inside their hotel rooms in Belgium.

Many were finding it difficult to drop off and the hotel's overpowering central heating system was being blamed for the lack of shut-eye on the eve of the big match.

Not that sleep was on Alan Cousin's mind.

'Big Cus', as he was affectionately known, was taking unpaid leave of absence from his teaching post to play in the European Cup. Cousin continued working while in Belgium and did so until late at night.

The following morning a bus carrying 34 supporters left Dundee at 5.30am for Renfrew Airport where a chartered plane would take them to Brussels. Among them was a 17-year-old woman who had never been to a football match before, didn't know who Dundee were playing or what the competition was!

Jute worker Maureen Thomson from Old Glamis Road had won the ticket in a prize draw and refused offers of up to £20 to part with it.

'My father, six of my eight brothers, and my boyfriend, are all Dundee daft,' she said. 'I've been offered everything from new coats to a series of hairdressing appointments for the ticket. But I've turned down the lot. I've always wanted to go abroad and to fly and the chance is too good to miss.'

She was the only female in the bus party and had been loaned a Dundee scarf by her brother so she could blend in.

Dundee's spy in Belgium was John Doorbar, a British embassy official in Brussels. Mr Doorbar had been watching Anderlecht and sending reports to Bob Shankly about the team and its tactics.

He said Anderlecht still had memories of the 10-0 defeat against Manchester United and were not happy to have drawn British opposition.

'I have seen Anderlecht regularly this season and there is no doubt that they have developed into one of the most attractive teams on the continent,' he said. 'They say they want to establish a three-goal lead to boost their confidence for their trip to Scotland. However, I feel it will be a very close game because Anderlecht can be very bad at times. Earlier this season they were held at home by the team at the very foot of the league.'

Dundee supporters were hoping for at least a draw to give them a good chance of winning the tie back at Dens.

Shankly's men were at full strength as the teams took to the field on Wednesday, 6 March in front of 64,703 noisy fans armed with bugles, rattles and firecrackers. That was near the stadium capacity and remains the biggest crowd ever for any football match in Belgium.

Anderlecht: Fazekas, Heylens, Cornelis, Hanon, Verbiest, Lippens, Janssens, Jurion, Stockman, Van Himst, Puis.

Dundee: Slater, Hamilton, Cox, Seith, Ure, Wishart, Smith, Penman, Cousin, Gilzean, Robertson.

Almost the entire senior schoolboy population of the Belgian capital was at the game in one part of the terracing, where they were being looked after by their teachers. There were also troops of Scouts and other youth bodies that had been given special cut-price admission to the game.

The Belgian hosts played 'The Dundee Song' by Hector Nicol over the public address system. The 200 Dundee fans sung along to the Dens Park anthem in which all of Dundee's team get a mention in the lyrics as a tribute to the title-winning heroes.

In a bizarre turn of events, the Dens Park anthem was followed immediately by 'The Tannadice Song' which was on the flip side. Steppé wasn't sure which one to play so he played both!

He wasn't the only one caught napping.

High up on a specially built, tiered platform, eight TV commentators from five countries were breaking out in a sweat. The Eurovision cameras were warming up but even as the whistle blew a voice said, 'Two minutes to go.' The TV cameras missed Alan Gilzean's quick-fire opening goal in 65 seconds.

Ure, Robertson, Smith, Penman, Cousin and Gilzean were all involved in the build-up. Gilzean took the return pass and struck a powerful low shot past Hungarian goalkeeper Árpád Fazekas to give Dundee a dream start.

Scotsport commentator Alex Cameron was on the gantry and he recalled the night the screens went blank in *The Scottish Football Book No 9* in 1963.

He said, 'On my right a Dutch commentator hurled angry words at the engineers. The Swiss on my left sat twitching nervously.'

And I wondered what *Scotsport* editor Arthur Montford was thinking as he studied the screens from

Glasgow. The play see-sawed. Anderlecht attacked. And then quite suddenly the ball was cleared upfield to Gordon Smith. Still the monitor sets beside us remained ominously blank.

'Smith looked up as he has done thousands of times before and prepared to cross. When he did, it was so accurate that the ball could have been aimed for a sixpence.

'Alan Gilzean saw the black object whirling towards him as if from floodlit space and couldn't believe his good fortune. He stepped forward alertly ... wham! ... and it was a goal, the first of four for Dundee. Exactly a minute had been played.

'My description of the goal was as detailed and colourful as I could make it in a state of mixed dejection and elation. For nobody heard it except a sound recorder who spoke Flemish.

'Thirty seconds later the commentators were told to "parlez, parlez" by a head-phoned character who was smirking his head off.

'On the earphones there was a garble of noise and talk. And laughter.

'Later I asked about the joke. The official I was told, was an ardent Anderlecht supporter. Solemnly he broke his resistance with: "Good, they've all missed the Dundee goal but we'll be in time all right for the ones by Anderlecht.'"

Gilzean's goal was one of just three Dundee shots on goal to Anderlecht's 14 in an action-packed first half as Dundee soaked up the pressure and hit the Belgians on the break.

Ian Ure was a rock for Dundee at the back as they defended their lead and his blond head was always at the ready for any ball which came his way. Bert Slater made three fantastic saves and Bobby Cox cleared off the line twice following Dundee's opening goal as the Belgians ramped up the pressure.

Gilzean then made Anderlecht pay for a string of missed chances on 18 minutes when he doubled Dundee's advantage with a magnificent goal. Cousin went out to the left wing and his cross was touched sideways by Robertson. Gilzean ran on and gave the goalkeeper no chance from 20 yards.

Anderlecht's only goal came from the penalty spot on 36 minutes when Cox was penalised for handball despite claiming it hit his chest. Belgium international Martin Lippens coolly dispatched the spot kick past Slater.

Dundee went in 2-1 up at the break and the players spoke in the dressing room about the prospect of beating a club which had eliminated Real Madrid.

Shankly, who was the master of understatement, remained calm and initially just stood in silence and started to light up a cigarette. Gilzean stood up and said, 'Boss, we've got them on the run. Just give the ball to Gordon [Smith] and he'll beat the full-back and cross to me at the far post. I'll just nod it in.'

Shankly took a big puff on his cigarette, looked up and said emphatically, 'It's all fine and well saying that, Gillie, but we just have to keep it simple!'

Dundee did keep it simple and stunned the Belgians with a third soon after the restart. Gilzean knocked down a Hamilton lob and Cousin was left with the easy job of netting.

The game was put beyond doubt on 71 minutes. Gilzean rose with Fazekas and the ball broke in front of an open goal. Smith stormed in from the wing and scored with his left foot. The goal appeared to knock the stuffing out of Anderlecht. Slater was seldom called upon for the remainder of the match.

The poor bloke who was in charge of Heysel Stadium's huge scoreboard display was also cursing

Dundee. He had to keep climbing up to replace the panels every time a goal was scored.

For the last ten minutes Dundee slowed the game down to walking pace and were happy to keep possession and run the clock down. Gilzean played on with an ankle injury that he had suffered after just 20 minutes and he went to hospital at full time to get the nasty gash stitched up.

At the final whistle, Dundee's noisy travelling support gave their players a tremendous reception. In their excitement some fans climbed the barriers around the pitch and carried goalkeeper Bert Slater shoulder-high. And, in the ultimate compliment to an outstanding performance, the Anderlecht fans gave Dundee a standing ovation.

Dundee had wiped the floor with Belgium's best and Slater's performance between the sticks earned even higher praise than his heroics in Cologne. He was the hero of the hour, although it was an accord that could equally be claimed by two-goal Alan Gilzean.

The travelling fans were jubilant and marched through the streets of Brussels after the match singing Dundee songs.

The incredible win also caused jubilant scenes back home in Dundee. The switchboard at *The Courier* was overwhelmed by calls from supporters. There were 150 calls from homes, clubs and pubs which increased in momentum as the evening went on. The half-time and final score announcements were also greeted with cheers at Dundee Business Club's annual dinner at the Invercarse Hotel.

In at least one city cinema the film was forgotten as the news flashed round the hall. One local producer also wondered what was going on. His theatre dress rehearsal was brought to a sudden halt after the stage manager whispered the news to the cast through the curtain.

Although there was no live coverage of the game in Scotland, many desperate fans back home in Dundee found a solution to the problem. They tuned into a Flemish radio station and followed the match by picking out the references to the Dundee names – and the silence that showed Dundee had scored. Hearing Cousin and Gilzean mentioned by a gloomy Belgian told them all they needed to know.

Dundee fans painted the town red in Brussels following the sensational victory. Among those in the away end was George Grant, who had travelled to all of Dundee's previous European away ties. He had taken the opportunity during his stay to visit former European boxing champion Jean Sneyers, who was now operating a big taxi firm in Brussels.

Dundee's 'Mr Boxing' was celebrating in the stand alongside newsagent George Boyd after watching his team land a punishing blow to Anderlecht's glory bid.

'Dundee must now be rated among the top teams in the world,' said George.

Arbroath miniature railway proprietor Matthew Kerr was another proud Dundee fan in the away end. Mr Kerr had also followed the team to Cologne and Lisbon. This time he had made his own last-minute arrangements. He travelled by train from Arbroath to London before going on the overnight ferry from Dover to Ostend and then on to Brussels.

AC Milan's manager Nereo Rocco was also in the crowd for the match and he said Dundee were now the best team left in the tournament. 'This is one team I am praying we shall not meet if we get to the final of the European Cup,' he said. 'They're a thousand times better than any of the other teams.'

Dundee chairman James Gellatly was completely overcome with emotion in the main stand at the final whistle. He said, 'We didn't expect such a fine win as this. It was a very sporting game and a complete credit to European football.'

The Dundee chairman reserved special praise for the performances of Slater and Ure.

Anderlecht manager Pierre Sinibaldi said Dundee deserved to win but he refused to concede the tie.

'Today's result does not necessarily mean we will be beaten in Dundee,' he said. 'But to make up three goals will of course be extremely difficult against such opponents.'

He described Ure as one of the best centre-halves he had ever seen and said he would be a success on the continent.

He said, 'It was Dundee's turn tonight. It could be ours next week. That is how football goes. Dundee came to keep the ball out of their goal and we must accept that they did their job exceptionally well. Had we reversed the goalkeepers we would not have been down 4-1.'

Anderlecht captain Martin Lippens urged his fans not to write his side off despite Dundee's three-goal advantage and said they could still overturn the deficit at Dens.

Likewise, his creative team-mate Joseph Jurion, whose mother had once run the canteen when he had previously played at Ruisbroek FC, remained convinced that they still had a chance of dining with Europe's best in the semi-final.

'Maybe Dundee will open up that defence for us by switching to an attacking game before their own people,' he said. 'I feel we have the speed and ball control to score on the break as they did to us. However, I honestly anticipate them being pleased to put the work on our shoulders by keeping at least two forwards deep enough to strengthen their defence.'

Trainer Sammy Kean said he was delighted with the stamina shown by his players which saw them outlast Anderlecht over the 90 minutes despite the heavy pitch. He said they looked amazingly fresh in the last quarter of the game despite their worrying lack of match practice over the past nine weeks.

Kean might have been delighted with the performance but he also played down talk that Dundee already had one foot in the next round with a three-goal advantage.

'As far as I'm concerned the second game starts off at 0-0,' he said. He added that Dundee would approach next Wednesday's return leg with a cautious attitude despite the result surpassing their wildest dreams.

Bobby Cox was still unhappy at the penalty decision and showed off the mud mark on his jersey where he claimed the ball had struck his chest rather than his arm. Gordon Smith said he was impressed by Anderlecht despite the scoreline. He reserved special praise for the mercurial teenage forward Paul Van Himst, stating that the Belgian international was 'certainly all he was cried up to be'.

'Smash and grab tactics had Belgians reeling', thundered *The Courier*'s headline. Having scored four goals 'with less than 20% of the play', chief football writer and ex-player Tommy Gallacher rightly identified Dundee's clinical finishing as key.

Asked for his post-match views, Bob Shankly said, 'It was a clash of styles and Anderlecht lost because they couldn't change their tactics. Before we came to Brussels we would have settled for a draw, but we took our chances, and, after all, that's football.'

The Dens boss said he had full confidence in his players but admitted he did not expect to win by such a margin. He said, 'They carried out the instructions I gave them before the match to the letter – let Anderlecht attack, and then counter-attack.'

The Dundee players were unanimous that a plan which was devised at the New York international tournament the previous summer was a huge factor in their win. Harsh lessons had been learned from adverse experiences against the two German sides over there.

After the 2-0 defeat to Reutlingen on Randall's Island, Dundee had again struggled to keep the ball against Saarbrücken in Detroit and lost 5-1.

Shankly decided Dundee's attacking style would have to be tempered and he and Kean had sown the seeds for the new counter-attacking style of play in Central Park, thereafter to be used in the European Cup.

As soon as they were under the slightest pressure, everyone was to get back, leaving just Alan Gilzean and Alan Cousin in the attacking third. They would put up a barrier around the 18-yard line and await their opportunity to counter-attack.

This was not a totally alien concept to the Dark Blues. Previously, they had done much the same but on an unplanned basis. One perfect example had been that foggy afternoon at Ibrox in November 1961. Dundee had broken from deep at speed with similarly deadly passing interchanges and Rangers had been utterly destroyed.

Now though, in Europe, it was a planned strategy and in Brussels it had worked to perfection.

'New York was the first time we came up against the continental-type defensive game,' said Cousin. 'We thought it was a terrible way to play football, but we learned from it, and now we are profiting. Quite honestly I'm not too surprised we're doing so well in the European Cup. I knew we had the football to get us this far. I only hope we can keep it up.'

The new system had put Dundee top of the heap and those little-town blues from earlier in the season were now melting away.

Dundee were making a brand new start of it and ripping apart Europe's best along the way.

Chapter 10

Tears of a Clown?

'Anderlecht were like a lovely wrist watch
– nice but not gold.'
Anderlecht general secretary Eugène Steppé

DUNDEE'S PLAYERS arrived at the after-match banquet to find Anderlecht goalkeeper Árpád Fazekas on a seat sobbing outside.

The Hungary international had been blamed for the defeat by his team-mates, who made their feelings clear in the dressing room after the match.

Joseph Jurion said, 'What chance did we have when Dundee had seven or eight men waiting across their goal area? We are being criticised for playing the ball too much and across the park but we just could not break through the Scottish defence.

'I thought the Dundee defensive game was quite admirable and as good as I have seen on the continent. If we had a goalkeeper like Slater it would have been so different. Surely Fazekas must be dropped for our next game in Dundee?'

Hungarian Fazekas, who began his professional career at Ujpest Budapest, played for Bayern Munich from 1957 to 1961 and was part of the first Bayern team to win the German Cup following a 1-0 win over Fortuna Düsseldorf in 1957. Then the goalkeeper signed for Hessen Kassel in Germany's second tier before joining Anderlecht in the summer of 1962.

Now the former Bayern Munich hero was public enemy number one in Brussels.

Alex Hamilton was having none of it when they stumbled upon Fazekas. He told him, 'You're going inside and you'll be sitting with us.'

The Scottish international right-back assured him that the defeat was not his fault and that other players in his side had not exactly set the heather alight. He also told him that Dundee would have beaten anybody on the night. The Belgian players couldn't believe it when Fazekas walked in and sat down with the Dundee team amid scowling stares from his own team-mates.

The Dundee players were each given a cigar box and silver cigarette lighter as a gift. Skipper Bobby Cox won an extra prize when his name was drawn from the hat in a raffle for the match ball signed by all the players.

Anderlecht general secretary Eugène Steppé said his side underestimated Dundee.

'I did not think they could play as they did,' he said. 'They played with their brains and their hearts all the time. Anderlecht were like a lovely wrist watch – nice but not gold.'

The Dundee party left Brussels at 11.30 the following morning to fly back to Turnhouse before receiving a great welcome from hundreds of fans at Tay Bridge Station.

Bob Shankly also had to deal with a bulging mailbag following the 4-1 victory with congratulatory letters arriving from home and abroad.

Alan Gilzean, meanwhile, was struggling to walk. The striker was Dundee's only casualty from the first leg.

His team-mates arrived at Dens for their usual Friday morning of light training following their midweek endeavours. Gilzean reported to the infirmary. His ankle wound, which received six stitches, was strapped up and he was immediately ruled out of Saturday's league match against Airdrie. His place in the team would be taken by Bobby Waddell.

Gilzean was also a doubt for the return leg against Anderlecht, for which over 26,000 tickets had already been sold.

Dundee suffered a European hangover in dismal conditions at Broomfield. They badly missed the talismanic Gilzean and a disappointingly small crowd of just 4,000 watched Airdrie defeat the league champions 1-0 in a mud-bath.

After such a huge effort in Brussels and the prospect of clinching a European Cup semi-final place just a few days away, this was not so surprising. In something of an understatement, Bert Slater declared, 'That was something of an anti-climax.'

Gilzean was still limping badly but Shankly was refusing to completely write off his chances of leading the line against Anderlecht on Wednesday.

The reserve game between Dundee and Airdrie also went ahead at Dens despite concerns over the damage it might inflict on the heavy pitch ahead of the return leg.

Shankly, for his part, said Dundee had no choice but to play the match. He said the reserves had already been starved of practice as a result of the Big Freeze and he needed them to be match-fit and match-sharp because they might be needed.

The pitch actually stood up well to the reserve game. Dens Park groundsman Jim Duncan worked late on Saturday night replacing all the divots by hand because it was too wet to use the roller.

In Belgium there was no surprise when goalkeeper Fazekas was dropped for the league game against Ghent. It had been made public that he wouldn't be in the team for the return game at Dens. He wouldn't even make the flight, such was the fury at his display.

Jean-Marie Trappeniers, 21, who was the regular first-choice goalkeeper during Anderlecht's title-winning season, had been recalled to the first team. Ironically, it was the fact he was so young that made Anderlecht sign Fazekas in the first place after they qualified for the European Cup.

His return was likely to be the only change in the team despite doubts over the fitness of right-back Georges Heylens and swashbuckling centre-forward Jack Stockman. Both had been injured in Sunday's match against Ghent although Heylens had battled back from worse afflictions after almost losing a leg to illness the previous year.

He had noticed his leg was red and swollen following a league game and went to hospital. He was diagnosed with phlebitis, a vein inflammation. The doctor told him his leg would have to be amputated and Heylens faced the dreadful prospect of losing a leg and his football career at the age of 21.

Understandably, the Anderlecht physio got a second opinion. Specialist Jean-Louis Hustin was able to cure the inflammation but predicted the defender would lose either his teeth or hair as a side-effect of the treatment. He lost his hair but retained his leg and wore a wig after being paid to do so by a wig manufacturing company.

His team-mate Stockman was fighting a losing battle to start the game. If he didn't make it, his place would go to 31-year-old Belgian international winger Richard Orlans, who had signed in the summer from Cercle Bruges. The decision over whether Heylens or Stockman would be risked in the return leg against Dundee was left to the players themselves.

Anderlecht were confident they could turn the tables at Dens after a morale-boosting win against

Ghent but Dundee were convinced they would finish the job.

The Dark Blue legions appeared to share that optimism and were ready to turn out in force. There were already 35,000 tickets sold compared with 25,000 for Cologne and 32,000 against Sporting Lisbon.

Around 150 Anderlecht supporters were due to arrive in Dundee, including 89 on a charter flight. The first nine supporters turned up in Dundee speaking little or no English and they also had nowhere to stay after travelling for over 24 hours.

They had left Brussels by train at 6am on Monday and arrived at 9am in Dundee on Tuesday, appealing to the *Evening Telegraph* to find accommodation for them. A dozen phone calls later they were safely installed in hotels after walking through the city centre in colourful scarves and hats. The same group had travelled to Glasgow the previous season to watch Standard Liege advance 4-3 on aggregate against Rangers in the European Cup.

More Anderlecht fans arrived, including men wearing bowler hats in club colours. Two supporters travelled all the way to Dundee in a car which had 'Dundee-Anderlecht' painted on the back and the slogan 'It's a long way to Wembley'. They were soon joined in the city by the Anderlecht party, which included 15 players, 12 officials, 20 journalists and nine supporters. The players and officials arrived resplendent in maroon blazers at Tay Bridge Station around 4.30pm on Tuesday having flown out from Brussels at 10am to London.

Manager Pierre Sinibaldi was in a confident mood but was concerned about the ability of his reserve players to step up if Heylens and Stockman were ruled out.

'It will definitely weaken the side if Heylens too is unable to play,' he said. 'Our reserves have not had match practice. They have only played in friendly games this season.

'Tactics? Our tactics will be not to make the mistakes we made last week. We will win. But three goals? That is a different matter.'

They were welcomed by Dundee chairman James Gellatly, director Robert Crichton, manager Bob Shankly and trainer Sammy Kean, along with a crowd of autograph hunters. Joseph Jurion, who arrived in his trademark glasses, was the main target of the fans that turned up at the station hoping to catch a glimpse of Anderlecht's star names.

The Belgians were booked into a hotel just 100 yards from the station but Anderlecht's first concern was to jump on a bus to inspect the Dens Park pitch. They had been told about the six to eight feet of difference between the two goals and some of them were under the impression they would be playing on the side of a hill!

Skipper Martin Lippens described the pitch as better than Heysel after a brief inspection proved their fears of playing up a slope were unfounded. 'We have absolutely no complaints – though we may have a few after the game,' he said.

The Anderlecht party then returned to their hotel for a quiet night. They were on a £350-a-man bonus to reach the semi-final and £65 for a win against Dundee.

Alan Gilzean had been joined on the treatment table by Ian Ure following the 1-0 defeat against Airdrie. Ure was a doubt after taking knocks on the shin and both ankles, but both men were hoping to be fit for the big game.

'My ankle is much better today,' said Gilzean. 'I am still limping, but, if it continues to make this progress I have a good chance of playing on Wednesday.'

Shankly confirmed that Bobby Waddell would deputise if Gilzean didn't make it. Gilzean was booked in for another appointment with the club doctor. Lawrie Smith wasn't too optimistic about Gilzean's chances of making it and described him as 'an average healer' but said they would 'have to wait and see'.

Later in the evening the Dundee officials returned to the station. They were there to meet Swiss referee Gottfried Dienst and his linesmen Alfred Steppacher and Albert Künzle. Dienst would be officiating his 36th match involving sides from different countries.

He played for FC Basel from 1932 to 1944 and amateur side FC Kleinhüningen until 1948, when a chronic knee problem resulted in a switch to refereeing. When not working as a supervisor in a Basel telephone company, he worked his way up through the divisions, refereeing his first match in the top Swiss league in 1953 and his first international match in 1957, when Scotland beat West Germany 3-1.

Big matches that followed included the 1961 European Cup Final in Berne and a World Cup semi-final in Chile in 1962, so Dienst had plenty of experience.

The officials were entertained later that evening by local referees before being given the by-now mandatory tour of Keiller's sweet factory in the city the following morning.

Eighty-nine Anderlecht supporters flew in on Wednesday on charter flights from Belgium. The travelling support ensured hotel rooms were in short supply in Dundee with some having to stay in Broughty Ferry and Arbroath.

Children from Clepington Primary, just across the road from Dens Park, were warned against attending the match because they had an 11-plus exam the following day.

Headmaster Charles Mowat said, 'I have pointed out that this is a very important exam. Their chances should not be jeopardised by catching a chill. The decision whether to go to the game is up to the individual boy and his parents.'

Leaflets, printed by supporters of rival clubs, were circulated in Brussels before the match, announcing the 'funeral arrangements' for Anderlecht after the return leg. The leaflets predicted that Anderlecht would be 'buried' in Scotland. 'No need to bring artificial flowers,' it added.

Gilzean arrived at Dens to undergo a rigorous late fitness test on the morning of the game. He was no longer walking with a limp and, although he was still feeling a bit of soreness, he was eager to play.

The big inside-left was eventually passed fit and would take his place in an unchanged side with a strapped-up ankle.

The six stitches inserted in Brussels were still in place. Dundee decided it was safer to keep them in rather than risk the injury re-opening if they were taken out in advance.

Gilzean, who had scored eight goals in five ties, was champing at the bit as he targeted the scoring record of the prolific Ferenc Puskas of Real Madrid, who held the record for a season in the European Cup having netted 12 goals in the 1959/60 competition.

The Coupar Angus man had already equalled the record for a British player, set by Manchester United's Dennis Viollet of the Busby Babes.

Anderlecht's centre-forward 'Dynamite Jack' was also passed fit after his injured ankle was given a massage in his hotel room. 'Yesterday I was crying with the pain,' said Stockman.

'Now I feel none.'

Georges Heylens, though, was ruled out at right-back after breaking down while being put through his paces on the Dens track in the morning.

His place in the Anderlecht side would be taken by young defender Jean Plaskie, making his European Cup debut.

Anderlecht didn't train before the match and instead went for a stroll through the centre of Dundee.

They tried to put the match to the back of their minds as they went hunting for souvenirs to take back home.

The bespectacled Jurion said Anderlecht were confident they would beat Dundee but he didn't think they could overturn the aggregate score.

'We are to go all out for goals in the first ten minutes,' he said.

'We can beat Dundee but I see no chance of pulling it off overall.

If they defend like that again, we will have some job breaking down their wall.'

Ian Ure stressed the importance of keeping things tight at the back in the early exchanges.

'What is more important is to ensure that Anderlecht don't get a quick goal to inspire them,' he said. 'After all, we have three goals in hand and time is on our side. It's Anderlecht who have to worry about getting goals.'

Ure said that didn't mean Dundee would park the bus and put up a defensive wall despite their three-goal advantage.

The match would take place in front of just over 38,000 fans, the biggest attendance at Dens since the ground record was broken by the 42,034 in a Scottish Cup tie against Rangers in February 1953.

Passengers taking the bus to the game were asked for identification as well as their names and addresses if they were unable to pay their fares. This was following a decision reached by the Dundee Transport Committee before the match in response to what was being described as 'an increasing problem'. Over the past 12 months over 1,000 passengers without cash had given their names and addresses but a third were found to be fictitious when transport staff called at the addresses.

Many of the crowd came from out of town to watch the European Cup quarter-final and Tay Bridge Station was described as 'like a battlefield'.

Aberdeen supporters were among those at Dens after travelling from Perth. They arrived at the station after watching their team's Scottish Cup win against St Johnstone. The Perth game had a 4.30pm kick-off, allowing the supporters to see both matches in the same day.

Many motorists parked half a mile or more from the ground and traffic arrangements worked smoothly despite the record attendance for a game under the lights.

Big crowds have a life of their own. You could see clouds of people's breath, lit cigarette ends and puffs of smoke coming from supporters all over the ground.

Scotland manager Ian McColl was among those watching from the main stand.

Dundee: Slater, Hamilton, Cox, Seith, Ure, Wishart, Smith, Penman, Cousin, Gilzean, Robertson.

Anderlecht: Trappeniers, Plaskie, Cornelis, Hanon, Verbiest, Lippens, Janssens, Jurion, Stockman, Van Himst, Puis.

Anderlecht needed a bright start to have any chance of progression but Alan Cousin should have had the game sewn up for Dundee within six minutes of kick-off.

Slater made a clearance which went straight down the middle of the park.

Alan Gilzean outjumped Verbiest and knocked it into the path of his strike partner.

Cousin was now through on goal. Trappeniers rushed out to narrow the angle. Cousin should have kept going but decided to strike the ball early. His weak shot from 16 yards trundled softly past the post.

Within two minutes the white and mauve maestros from Brussels almost took the lead themselves in what was a topsy-turvy start. Big Stockman's strike from 18 yards was brilliantly saved by Slater.

But the Dundee goalkeeper couldn't hold the ball. It rebounded towards Wilfried Puis who stabbed it towards goal, only to watch it being cleared off the line by the knee of Bobby Cox with Slater beaten. Hanon shot over the bar for Anderlecht on 14 minutes.

Both sides were looking good in the early exchanges, although Dundee's passing left a lot to be desired. A colour clash saw several passes from Dundee players land directly at the feet of referee Gottfried Dienst, who was also wearing dark socks.

On 20 minutes Bobby Wishart took matters into his own hands and beat three men through the middle before finding Robertson, who couldn't finish. Anderlecht were playing some fabulous football under the floodlights. On 29 minutes the early Belgian pressure paid off and they went in front when Ian Ure was pulled out of position by Paul Van Himst.

He flicked the ball over Hamilton's head and the unmarked Stockman smashed it into the roof of the net from 12 yards to give his team a glimmer of hope and silence the large Dens Park crowd.

Dundee went straight up the park and might have had a penalty when full-back Plaskie appeared to bundle Robertson off the ball inside the box. The referee gave Dundee an indirect free kick which came to nothing.

Alan Gilzean was not looking as sharp as he did in some of the previous games but he was still taking two opposition defenders with him wherever he went. On 38 minutes Dundee's main goal threat was fouled on the edge of the box. He took the free kick himself but his strike was wild.

Dundee kept up the pressure and Penman was put through on goal by Robertson but the Anderlecht goalkeeper managed to kick the ball from his feet. Five minutes before the break a Stockman header from close range went high over the bar and Dundee struck the woodwork at the other end. A Cousin lob from 20 yards was tipped against the bar by Trappeniers, who recovered quickly to poke the ball away with Gilzean diving at full stretch for the rebound.

Dundee went in a goal down at half-time but were still 4-2 ahead on aggregate. They were the more aggressive side after the interval and went looking for the quick goal which would put the tie out of sight.

A Gordon Smith strike flew past the post straight from kick-off and the home side kept up the pressure for the next 15 minutes with wave after wave of attack.

First, Gilzean failed to connect with a Smith cross before Robertson hooked a shot wide from 20 yards. Dundee were then awarded a free kick on the 18-yard line which was deflected for a corner. Robertson collected Smith's cross but fired straight across the goal.

On 61 minutes Cousin set off on a great run. He beat two defenders and cut the ball back for Gilzean who managed to get his foot to it, but the goalkeeper dived across the line and kept it out.

Smith was now coming more and more into the game. His brothers Stanley and Willie were watching in the crowd. Stanley had flown over from Toronto and arrived in time to watch Dundee's 1-0 league defeat by Airdrie and thought he would never see the team score.

Another shot from Smith went just past the post. Penman was next to go through alone as the home pressure continued to mount.

Dundee gathered strength in the closing stages as the Belgian champions ran out of fuel on the wide, open spaces of the Dens pitch. Smith's habit of pulling the ball back and crossing with his left foot continued to prove a thorn in the side for Jean Cornelis, who was constantly troubled.

The pressure paid off on 78 minutes. Smith crossed and Gilzean went up for the ball with two Belgian defenders. The ball broke to Cousin, who swept it low into the net from 18 yards. The goalkeeper was beaten all the way.

Cheers and songs rang round the ground as Dundee's semi-final place was all but assured. The atmosphere inside the ground was electric and the timeless Smith capped his display with a glorious winner just four minutes later.

It started with a long ball from Hamilton to Robertson. There was a one-two with Penman before

Robertson's cross found Smith on the right 15 yards out. Smith struck the inside of the far post with his left-foot shot with Trappeniers stranded out of position.

The goal was described by *The Courier*'s Tommy Gallacher as 'a gem that will be recalled for many a day'.

A minute later Gilzean was clean through and missed an easy chance from near the penalty spot when he tried a flick and his shot was saved.

Gilzean was in amongst it again near the death. Four minutes from time, Robertson crossed for Penman. He knocked the ball on for Gilzean who put the ball in the net. But the flag went up for offside.

Anderlecht were down and out and they had only had one direct effort on target to trouble Bert Slater in the second half, in the last minute.

A few hundred fans ran on to the pitch at the end of the match to congratulate the players but were quickly directed away by the police. A few spectators were so overcome by the excitement of it all that they had to receive medical treatment. There was tragedy amongst the triumph, however, when 72-year-old Ralph Chalmers from Arbroath collapsed and died while watching the match with his brother-in-law.

The big drummer of the pipe band which played before the match joined in the celebrations by beating his drum in front of the stand. The fans lapped it up and clapped and stamped to the drum beat!

The Dundee Telephone Exchange was under just as much pressure as the drum after receiving inquiries during the match about the score from across Britain.

Thousands of ecstatic supporters then poured out into the dimly lit streets. It was damp and cold with small remnants of snow in places, but no one cared. Cup fever saw evening classes at Dundee Technical College being much lighter than usual with just nine out of the usual 37 students turning up for class.

The Dundee directors threw the traditional banquet for the Anderlecht team, officials and the members of the Belgian press who had covered the match. Dundee chairman James Gellatly handed over a silver salver to the Anderlecht president at the Royal British Hotel. The Belgian players and directors received a tartan travelling rug similar to the gift Bobby Wishart had turned his nose up at back in 1955!

'It is easy to be gracious when you are winning but the true test of sportsmanship is to be gracious when things don't go your way,' said Mr Gellatly. 'Anderlecht have certainly upheld their name of Royal Sporting Club in this tie.'

Anderlecht president Albert Roossens said Dundee were unknown when the draw was made but now he was predicting they could go all the way to the Wembley final.

He also paid tribute to the Dens Park crowd for the way they conducted themselves.

'They are very sporting indeed,' he said. 'I have never heard a crowd so solidly behind their own team with such fervour but at the same time so appreciative of the other team's efforts.'

Mr Roossens then surprised the Dundee officials by presenting the club with an inscribed piece of silverware bearing the Anderlecht crest.

Lord Provost Maurice McManus also congratulated Dundee and paid tribute to the sportsmanship of the Belgians.

Anderlecht general secretary Eugène Steppé said Shankly's side were better over the two games than Real Madrid and should fear no one in the semi-final.

'You have so much strength and spirit that I will back you against any of the others in the semi-final,' he said. 'We did not get our early goal and after that we did score but we did not hit hard enough for more before half-time.'

Mr Steppé said it was 'that man again' Bobby Cox who came out of the game with the most credit.

'He broke our hearts with his goal-line clearance in Brussels,' he said. 'In the eighth minute he did it again. If we had scored that one I think we may have had Dundee rattled.'

For his part, Belgian ace Jurion believed Dundee were the best club team he had ever played against and he didn't see any reason why they couldn't win the European Cup.

'Ure is tremendous and Bobby Cox is great,' he said. 'I can't see anyone stopping Dundee in the European Cup, not even Benfica.'

Dundee were joined in the semi-final draw by AC Milan, Benfica and Feyenoord. Belgian sportswriters reserved praise for Dundee's performance but suggested they didn't have enough quality to reach the final.

The French-language paper *Les Sports* said Anderlecht were defeated by 'the pace of the strong Scots' and described Dundee as a 'good team, capable of switching from deep defence to the broadest attack with great mastery'. *Le Peuple* told its readers that Dundee were a good team that was far-sighted with the ability to shoot well but would 'probably not go further in the cup'.

Bobby Seith didn't agree and believed Dundee could go all the way to Wembley.

He said, 'There's no limit to what we can do with Bob Shankly as manager. He treats every player alike and can't do enough to make you feel at ease. I've developed a great understanding with Ian [Ure] and Bobby Wishart alongside me and Alex Hamilton behind me. That understanding and the team spirit manager Bob Shankly has brought to the side are the reasons for our success.

'Now I think we can do what no British club has ever done – go to the European Cup Final. I honestly believe we can beat any of the three sides left in the competition – Benfica, Milan and Feyenoord. I'm sure we'd all like to meet Benfica in the semi, so that we can beat either of the other two in the final. Who knows? We might even make it a double this season, the European Cup and the Scottish Cup.'

Dundee were a team in demand following their new-found fame with offers expected to pile in from clubs trying to 'cash in' with the offer of a friendly match.

The papers were full of it. Anderlecht's rivals Standard Liege were reportedly ready to be the first to make such an offer by inviting Dundee back to Belgium.

Shankly admitted he was expecting there would be offers but ruled out a summer tour because he wanted to give his players a break from competition.

'Invitations must be expected now that we have reached the last four of the European Cup,' he said. 'But I'd be against any tours this summer. We had three weeks in America last year and this has been a very hard season for us. I'd prefer the players to get a break from football this year.'

The Anderlecht players and officials said it with flowers as they left Tay Bridge Station for Turnhouse Airport the following morning, buying a huge bunch of flowers and presenting the blooms and a signed photograph of the Anderlecht team to James Gellatly's wife before leaving. The party was also seen off by Mr Gellatly and Robert Crichton.

A 59-year-old Dundee postman received just as many compliments later in the day after being the hero of a lunchtime blaze in the city's Kirkton estate. He snatched two young children from certain death when fire raged through a semi-detached house in Forres Crescent. Despite dense smoke and flames, Percy Ham risked his life by going back into the house after rescuing the younger child. After the interruption to his round, Mr Ham continued with his deliveries and finished on time!

Dundee also returned to the day job in fine fashion when they defeated strong-going Partick Thistle 2-1 at Dens Park just a few days after completing the destruction of Anderlecht.

Naturally, though, it was Dundee's continental exploits that had astounded the football world. In real Roy of the Rovers style, they sat high and dry in the last four of the European Cup. All eyes would now turn to the semi-final draw which was about to take place in Amsterdam.

Ian Ure believed Dundee could go all the way.

He said, 'The edge seems to have gone slightly from our league games but if we can find the form we had in our earlier games we can win the competition.'

The Dens Park club had exceeded all expectations and now they lay at the edge of greatness.

Chapter 11

Meet the Mad King of Catenaccio

'Who are they and are they as good as
Tottenham?'

Milan secretary Bruno Passalacqua

DUNDEE'S AMBITIONS for the rest of the season were not just confined to the European Cup.

An Alan Gilzean header brought victory over Hibernian at Dens to earn a mouth-watering Scottish Cup quarter-final clash with league leaders Rangers at the end of March. It was another home tie and Dundee hoped they might again rise to the big occasion and go on to Scottish Cup glory.

Attention, though, quickly returned to the European Cup campaign.

Dundee chairman James Gellatly flew to Amsterdam for the semi-final draw on 26 March and saw the Dark Blues paired with AC Milan. It was the draw Dundee wanted to avoid. The Italian aces were formidable opponents.

The first game was to be played in Italy on 24 April, the return leg on 1 May.

Cup holders Benfica, meanwhile, drew Feyenoord of Rotterdam. The Dutch side were not then the force they later became in the 1970s and were seen by many as the weakest of the four remaining clubs.

Mr Gellatly put a brave face on things.

'We did not mind who we got,' he said. 'At this stage they are all good teams. It was going to be hard whoever we were drawn against, but this is certainly a tough one. My only concern is that we play the first match away.'

However, José Crahay, general secretary of the Royal Belgian Football Association, chairman of the European Cup organising committee and a co-founder of UEFA, had some words of encouragement.

He believed Milan were not unbeatable and highlighted the outstanding contribution of defender Ian Ure in Dundee's run to the semi-final.

'With such a man on your side, just about anything is possible,' he said. 'I was hugely impressed by him at Heysel. Taking a really competent player as my guide, I would say he is three men in one. I think Dundee will be very fortunate if they are able to keep him for I know he is greatly fancied by the big clubs in both Spain and Italy.'

There was a more quizzical expression on the sun-tanned face of Milan secretary Bruno Passalacqua.

'Where is Dundee?' he asked. 'Who are they and are they as good as Tottenham?'

Many managers now studied or 'spied' on their opponents, but Bob Shankly disagreed with the concept.

'Nobody knows better than me that this is an important game for the club,' he said, 'but we've had dozens of big matches these past two seasons and I haven't gone scuttling around watching everyone we were due to meet. A team can play one way one day and quite another the next depending on the opposition.

'I could very easily confuse myself and I don't want to confuse my players. Nor do I want them overly focused on one particular match. I prefer my team to approach every game in the same frame of mind. It's time enough to start getting wound-up when we get to Milan.'

Former hospital physio Lawrie Smith agreed. 'When treating patients I had to be careful not to communicate any concerns to them. Dealing with highly trained players is not so very different so I'm all for the boss's idea of playing it cool.'

Milan manager Nereo Rocco, though, had watched Dundee against Anderlecht in Brussels and indicated there would be no complacency from his side.

'Dundee impressed me,' he said. 'They were full out for 90 minutes and never flagged.'

In his playing career, Rocco had mostly performed as a winger for Triestina, Napoli and Padova, making almost 300 appearances in Serie A with a single cap for the Azzurri in 1934.

Turning his hand to management, Rocco led his local club Triestina to second place in Serie A in 1947/48, their highest-ever placing, before later managing Treviso and Padova. In 1961, Rocco got his big chance with AC Milan after manager Gipo Viani, who guided them to league titles in 1956/57 and 1958/59, suffered a heart attack. Viani moved upstairs and Rocco took charge, promptly leading the Rossoneri to Serie A success in 1961/62.

The powerfully built Milan supremo was a strict disciplinarian who had built his side around four outstanding international players: Cesare Maldini, an imposing 33-year-old centre-half and team captain; left-half Giovanni Trapattoni; the brilliant young inside-left Gianni Rivera and centre-forward José Altafini.

Another international who recently featured in Milan was England striker Jimmy Greaves. In April 1961, the chirpy Cockney with electric pace had become the 'Hammer of the Scots' by netting a hat-trick in England's 9-3 Home International victory over Scotland. That June, Milan paid Chelsea £80,000 for their prolific goalscorer but, although he started impressively with nine goals in his opening 12 games, the move did not work out.

Other Brits plying their trade in Italy included John Charles, the Welsh international centre-half or centre-forward, who had a lucrative and highly successful career with Juventus between 1957 and 1962. Likewise England forward Gerry Hitchens in his spell with Inter Milan, Torino and Atalanta between 1961 and 1967.

However, in common with other highly talented but mercurial characters like Denis Law and Joe Baker – both at Torino for 1961/62 – Greaves rebelled against the rigid and somewhat oppressive discipline and quickly fell foul of Rocco's regime.

All three were to have but a short sojourn in Italy, with the Turin pair moving on to Manchester United and Arsenal, and Greaves sold to Tottenham Hotspur for £99,999 in December 1961 despite his impressive goals tally in Italy.

Greaves had played against Alan Gilzean and Hugh Robertson at Pittodrie in 1962 when he scored twice in a 4-2 win for England against Scotland in an Under-23 international.

'I had my brushes with Rocco,' admitted Greaves. 'He looks hard and he's tough, but he is very much what is required in Italy. I would not say that the Milan players train as hard as British players. It's a far more relaxed type of training. But they do have strict rules.

'If you are away for a training session and breakfast is laid on for 9am – this means 9am on the dot. No player is allowed to come down a minute late. Everything has to be done on schedule.'

Milan had their own hotel and training complex on the outskirts of the city where players were often taken before a match.

'There, they think and talk nothing but football,' said Greaves. 'This is down to Rocco and he makes sure it works. How long the team spend in that restricted environment depends on the importance of the match. For lesser games the players might not go to the hotel at all and instead be ordered to report straight to the ground. For other matches it might be up to three nights, perhaps a week before the match.

'But for Dundee I feel sure that Rocco will order a week in the wilds for the Milan team. His word is law. I've known him not to shave for three days. Then he looks tougher than ever!'

Greaves had played alongside centre-forward José Altafini, then regarded as the finest forward in Italy. Altafini was now in his fifth season at the San Siro and was a huge success with over 100 goals to his name.

The centre-forward had been part of Brazil's World Cup-winning squad in Sweden in 1958. Remarkably, he returned to the World Cup in Chile in 1962 wearing the famous blue jersey of Italy, his ancestral home.

Back then, Brazil had a policy of never calling on players once they went overseas and, similar to Real Madrid pair Alfredo di Stefano and Ferenc Puskas, who respectively switched from Argentina and Hungary to Spain, Altafini received FIFA dispensation permitting him to switch allegiance to Italy.

Greaves had been replaced by another Brazilian international, Dino Sani from Boca Juniors. From Sani's debut against Juventus, Milan took 31 points from the next 34 available to win the title. Sani was a clever and creative inside man. His partnership with Altafini and Rivera became highly productive.

Rocco gained a reputation perfecting the 'catenaccio' defensive system but his Serie A-winning side had netted an impressive 83 goals in 34 games. Milan's route to the European Cup semi-final had also included a couple of high-scoring victories.

In the preliminary round, Luxembourg minnows Union Sportif were hammered 14-0 on aggregate, with Galatasary of Turkey handed an 8-1 drubbing over the two legs of the quarter-final. Not to be outdone by Alan Gilzean's double hat-trick feat, José Altafini had managed three hat-tricks including eight goals in the two ties against Sportif.

There was encouragement for Dundee, however, as Alf Ramsey's Ipswich, the English champions – with Scots players Ray Crawford and Jimmy Leadbitter in their line-up – had pushed the Italians much closer in the intervening round. They went down 4-2 on aggregate having given themselves a mountain to climb after losing 3-0 in the San Siro.

Like Dundee, Milan's league form had been none too impressive either. They had managed just 45 goals in 29 league games, with Altafini accounting for just eight of those.

The lowdown on Dundee's newest and most glamorous opponents to date was provided by local newspapers like *The Courier*, the *Evening Telegraph* and the *People's Journal*. And, with nearly a month's wait until the semi-final ties, it was all eagerly digested by the Dundee footballing public and further afield too.

Now, though, the Dark Blues faced their biggest challenge of their domestic season with a Scottish Cup quarter-final at Dens Park. The visit of Rangers, as ever, was of huge interest and almost 37,000 turned out to witness a thriller in the rain.

It finished 1-1 and there was controversy when referee Barclay disallowed what appeared to be the winner for Rangers with two minutes remaining, amidst wild protests by the visiting players.

On Monday, the *Scottish Daily Mail* headline read 'Dundee are not tough enough'.

Mail columnist Bob Brian wrote, 'The moral of this story is that it takes more than skill to make a good cup team.

'It's imperative that Dundee learn this before the replay at Ibrox on Wednesday. Rangers already know it as they pointed out at Dundee on Saturday and because of it, they are the favourites for the semi-finals.

'Toughness – that's the password in the cup. Dundee have all the necessary skill but not the determination of Rangers. If they had there would be no replay.'

An accompanying picture showed a mass of empty beer bottles alongside the Dens Park boundary wall, saying: 'At 3d a time Dundee should make a good thing out of this lot of empties. This is only a fraction of the "dead men" collected after the Rangers tie at Dens.'

Bob Shankly's men, however, were fully concentrated on the Ibrox replay which came three days later.

Both teams were unchanged with Dundee again fielding their strongest side.

Dundee: Slater, Hamilton, Cox, Seith, Ure, Wishart, Smith, Penman, Cousin, Gilzean, Robertson.

Rangers: Ritchie, Shearer; Caldow, Greig, McKinnon, Baxter, Henderson, McLean, Millar, Brand, Wilson.

The tie attracted a crowd of almost 82,000 before the gates were shut.

Remarkably, it was Rangers' highest home attendance of the season, a couple of thousand higher than their European Cup Winners' Cup tie against Tottenham in December. It was a clear testimony to the high regard this Dundee side of the early 1960s was held in.

This time, Dundee showed plenty of fighting spirit and no lack of punch in attack only for uncharacteristic defensive errors to cost them dear.

It was a night of misery for Alex Hamilton. After 15 minutes a long, high ball caused indecision in the Dens defence and the right-back headed past Bert Slater, who had left his goal.

Alan Gilzean nodded the equaliser from a free kick on 34 minutes then burst through to shoot Dundee into the lead 30 seconds after half-time. With 17 minutes remaining Dundee led 2-1, looked comfortable and almost got a third when Gilzean's shot was cleared off the line by Shearer. But then Hamilton brought down Davie Wilson in the box.

Brand converted the spot kick and, with Rangers' tails up and backed by the huge crowd inside Ibrox, the inside-left spun clear of Ure to strike the winner right at the death.

Around 700 Dundee supporters were among those turned away by police with the ground already full. They circled the ground looking in vain for a way in before eventually giving up and heading home on the 9.30pm train.

Their misery was compounded when one of the diesel locomotives broke down and delayed their departure by an hour. Things didn't get much better when the train finally arrived in Dundee and it took almost an hour to clear the huge queue for taxis.

The route from Glasgow to Aberdeen would be different in the future after Dr Beeching's report on the reshaping of Britain's railways was finally published. There were 1,928 stations earmarked to close and 266 passenger services to be withdrawn, totalling about 5,000 route miles to save between £115m and £140m.

The Perth-Coupar Angus-Forfar-Kinnaber (near Montrose) line was axed in favour of the alternative Perth–Dundee–Aberdeen route, leaving the railway stations at Forfar and Coupar Angus redundant and set to fade into history.

Dundee's Alex Hamilton and Ian Ure would have a swift reunion with four of their erstwhile Ibrox foes following the cup defeat. Just three days later, on 6 April, the Dens duo lined up for Scotland against England on a gloriously sunny day at Wembley.

Scotland: Brown (Tottenham), Hamilton (Dundee), Caldow (Rangers), Mackay (Tottenham), Ure (Dundee), Baxter (Rangers), Henderson (Rangers), White (Tottenham), St John (Liverpool), Law (Manchester United), Wilson (Rangers).

England: Banks (Leicester City), Armfield (Blackpool), Byrne (Liverpool), Flowers (Wolves), Norman (Tottenham), Moore (West Ham), Douglas (Blackburn), Greaves (Tottenham), Smith (Tottenham), Melia (Liverpool), Charlton (Manchester Utd).

It was a disastrous afternoon for Scotland skipper Eric Caldow, who suffered a broken leg in a collision with Bobby Smith after just six minutes. But ten-man Scotland overcame the setback. Inspired by half-backs Dave Mackay and Jim Baxter – the latter of whom netted a quick-fire double – they went on to record one of their most famous victories.

It was a display of courage, skill and teamwork. Every Scot was a hero.

Dundee could take great pride from the presence of two of their players in the winning side. Hamilton bounced back from his lapses at Ibrox to keep a tight rein on the ever-dangerous Manchester United forward Bobby Charlton, while Ure had produced an almost impeccable display.

BBC commentator Kenneth Wolstenholme was fulsome in his praise for Ure, who he described as 'the greatest centre-half in the world today'.

Indeed Ure's performance was watched by representatives of many European clubs including Gigi Peronace, the well-known Italian agent who had lured Denis Law and Joe Baker to Torino in 1961.

While basking in the afterglow of Scotland's second successive victory over the Auld Enemy, Dundee's league form continued to give cause for concern. Successive defeats by Celtic, Queen of the South and

Hibernian did little to change the growing feeling that Dundee were saving themselves for the European Cup.

But veteran winger Gordon Smith hit back at the suggestion. He said, 'Dundee have been able to build football culture. With it the fans have enjoyed goals in the European Cup, and now, because we are not getting the breaks and goals, the fans are all upset.

'I don't think we have played better than we did against Rangers at Ibrox. We gave them a goal start and took the lead. The final result was one of the biggest disappointments of my career because we played them into the ground that night.

'At Dumfries and again in the game with Hibs we had all the pressure and lost. Don't let anyone say we are not trying. Because of our position every team is after our scalp. They defend in strength to keep us out then score in the break-away. It can happen to everybody in this game and it is pretty sad but we will strike again.'

Furthermore, Dens skipper Bobby Cox believed the run of defeats from struggling sides near the bottom of the table had done nothing to undermine their confidence.

He said: 'The lads are not downhearted although we would welcome one or two good wins before going to Italy. I think we have outplayed all the sides that beat us.'

Benfica were now looking likely opponents for Dundee or Milan in the final.

The first leg of their semi-final against Feyenoord took place in Rotterdam. It ended 0-0 in front of 51,000 fans. The Dutch looked the better team on the night but both sides missed several chances to win.

The Portuguese would have home advantage in the decider and looked strong favourites to go on and reach their third successive final.

Could Dundee turn the tide and join them at Wembley?

Chapter 12

Bobby Cox and the
Magic Lamp

'Apart from his presence helping the morale,
his determination is always a valuable
asset when it's most needed.'

Bob Shankly

DUNDEE BOUNCED back with a convincing 5-1 home win over St Mirren on 13 April. Bobby Waddell scored three and was now knocking on the door for a place in the team at the San Siro.

The St Mirren victory at Dens was watched by Milan assistant Nils Liedholm, a club legend who had won four league titles during his playing days there and captained Sweden in their run to the World Cup Final in 1958. He gave his verdict after the match and said that he was particularly impressed with the showings of Ian Ure, Gordon Smith and Alan Gilzean.

'Dundee are a good side and Milan will find it difficult here,' he said. The Swede said the general feeling within the Milan camp was that the winners of the trophy would come from the Milan–Dundee semi-final.

Waddell apart, there was further encouragement when Kenny Cameron netted four goals in a reserve game against Dundee United. Reserve-team skipper Alex Stuart, who played three games in the championship-winning season, was also having a great campaign. He was said to be improving with every game and gaining a reputation for having the best left foot in the business.

Tickets for the second leg of the Milan tie were now a hot topic of debate after going on sale following the St Mirren victory. Prices for the Dens return had prompted a backlash from some fans.

The home club kept all the gate money in the European Cup but thus far Dundee's opponents had all done better financially with bigger gates in Cologne, Lisbon and Brussels, all larger stadia than Dens Park.

Some thought the club was entitled to cash in on its success. Others suggested the Dens prices were a bit hard on pensioners who couldn't stand on the terracing and would have to pay either £1 10s or £2 for a seat. Dundee were also charging 7/6 for ground tickets and 12/6 for the enclosure.

When Ipswich entertained AC Milan in the second round they had charged 11/ – and 15/ – for a seat and 5/ – or 6/ – to stand under cover. Back then their Portman Road stadium had a capacity of 25,000.

Tottenham Hotspur were raising their prices for their upcoming European Cup Winners' Cup semi-final against OFK Belgrade with seats at 20/, 25/- and 30/-. That was no real surprise though. It was the same scale they had operated for the European Cup semi-final against Benfica the previous season.

It was still nothing compared to Italy, though, where travelling Dundee fans would soon discover that football was much more expensive. The average ticket for league football was 10/3 with a top ticket price of £6!

Milan had also fixed ticket prices for the first leg at the San Siro where they expected an 80,000 sell-out.

Their best stand seats cost the equivalent of £2-17-6d with ground tickets available at 9/3.

The build-up was continuing apace. The BBC *Sportsview* team including Kenneth Wolstenholme arrived at Dens to do some filming and interview the players for a special programme. *Sportsview*, the BBC's flagship sports magazine show, was presented by Peter Dimmock, the face of BBC Sport.

Eight inches of snow then fell during the Easter holiday weekend in Dundee with the AA describing it as 'utter and complete chaos' and 'unprecedented'. Just as chaotic was Dundee's midweek defeat to city rivals United. The Dark Blues were dumped 2-1 for the Tannadice side's first success at Dens since May 1951 when they won 3-2 in the final of the Forfarshire Cup.

Shankly was furious and said the match should have been stopped at half-time as the 22 players slipped and slithered around in the mud. The start was delayed by 15 minutes to allow fans in after the turnstiles were closed because Dundee officials were so pessimistic about the chances of the game going ahead.

The previous August, Dundee had avenged their opening-day derby defeat at Tannadice when a Gordon

Smith double brought a 2-1 Dens win over Dundee United in the League Cup. Both games had been contested in warm, sunny conditions.

Now, though, referee Tom 'Tiny' Wharton allowed the game to proceed despite a waterlogged pitch and refused to listen to several appeals to stop the game in the second half.

Both teams had to change into dry strips during the interval.

Conditions were impossible for the players and they walked off at the final whistle through ankle-deep water and mud.

The incessant rain made a complete mockery of the game and Shankly was understandably not a happy man.

'The game should have been abandoned at half-time when neither side had an advantage,' he said.

'There was doubt about the game even starting. It was much worse after the interval.'

United forward Neil Mochan, who played for Scotland in the 1954 World Cup in Switzerland, then recalled another game that was even worse.

'Ridiculous conditions, but I have played in worse and it was at Dens Park in March 1958 when I was left-back for Celtic,' he said. 'Dundee beat us 5-3. There was far more water and it was freezing cold. Our teeth were chattering at half-time and I remember a shivering Billy McPhail pleading in the dressing room that nobody would want us to go out again in such conditions.'

Dundee right-back Alex Hamilton had also played in that game but he thought the Dens derby conditions had been worse. He said, 'It was difficult to imagine a worse surface for football. We were sending balls six yards with full-blooded kicks. The game should have been stopped when there was no improvement in sight after the interval.'

Goalkeeper Bert Slater concurred, saying said it was the worst conditions he had ever played in during his professional career which had started in 1953.

The continual refusal to abandon was an astonishing decision by the legendary whistler Wharton and particularly bad luck for Dundee.

That luck was not to get much better.

In the following fixture at Motherwell, the 2-1 losing scoreline was repeated. Even worse was the knee injury sustained by Dens skipper Bobby Cox.

He was limping badly and there were fears that the left-back had a damaged cartilage that could rule him out of the first leg of the European Cup semi-final in Milan four days later. To add to Shankly's woes, Craig Brown, who would have been Cox's natural successor at left-back, pulled a leg muscle in the reserve game at Dens.

It was a huge blow for Cox, who also looked set to be called up by Scotland for their friendly against Austria at Hampden on 8 May. Despite his success with Dundee, Cox had never been capped for Scotland and Caldow's leg break against England looked to have opened the door for him. Now the 29-year-old Dens stalwart was struggling to be fit for two of the biggest matches of his career.

Meanwhile, as Dundee sweated over the fitness of their influential skipper, Milan had played out a goalless draw away from home against Torino in Serie A. Gianni Rivera and Dino Sani were rested, as was goalkeeper Giorgio Ghezzi who was recovering from a slight injury.

Torino, whose attack was led by England centre-forward Gerry Hitchens, played with only ten men for the second half after losing a player through injury.

It was clear that Milan had used the game as a warm-up with José Altafini saying, 'This was a training session before meeting Dundee. I preferred not to exert myself too much.'

The Rossoneri now lay fourth behind Inter, Juventus and Bologna. They were struggling to score goals and would spend the next two days trying to remedy things at their practice ground outside the city.

Cox was feeling more optimistic than the Dens medical staff.

'It's a wee bit stiff but there's no pain and no swelling,' he said. 'There's plenty time yet but it will really all depend on how the knee reacts when I kick a ball again.'

Cox said he would be having extensive treatment when he got to Milan. Shankly had agreed to give his skipper the last word on his fitness.

A Dickson's coach set off from Dundee for Milan on Sunday with 26 fans on board and cheered by around 50 well-wishers. A 500-mile overnight trip to Dover was the first leg of the journey. At noon on Monday they would board a ferry to Calais, then there would be an overnight stop in Epinal before pressing on via Basle, Lucerne and the Gotthard Pass to Faido. Wednesday would bring a short hop through Como and finally arrival in Milan at midday. The return trip would start at midnight after the match with the party due back in Dundee on Saturday morning. All in, the package cost £32.

Dundee's own journey to Milan started on Monday morning. The players, management and officials were cheered on by over 100 fans when they boarded the train to Edinburgh where they were due to fly from Turnhouse. The Dundee party was joined on the station platform by Tommy Neilson, Jimmy Irvine and Alex Gordon from Dundee United, who arrived to wish them luck.

Shankly decided he would hold off announcing his team until the afternoon of the match and everybody in the party was hoping Cox would be fit to lead out Dundee.

'We are anticipating a very hard game,' said Shankly. 'I don't think it will be another Cologne, but it will probably be the nearest to it for toughness. That's why I'm a lot happier that Bobby Cox still feels he'll make it. Apart from his presence helping the morale, his determination is always a valuable asset when it's most needed.'

Cox had suffered a similar injury on his other knee two years previously but, after undergoing an operation, was back playing six weeks later in Dundee's 1961 summer tour to Iceland. The captain was so desperate to play that he was carrying his own treatment lamp on the 1,000-mile journey to Italy.

On arrival at Edinburgh's Waverley station the Dundee party were joined by Bert Slater, Doug Houston, Andy Penman, Gordon Smith and Alan Cousin. From there it was on to a special bus to Turnhouse Airport where they were met by a yelling band of 'Mexican bandits' who were carrying ropes and demanding money.

The reception committee was a group of Edinburgh University students who were dressed up for RAG week and were raising money for various charities. Every player was forced to stump up some cash when they left the bus. Handing over the ransom demand still didn't stop Ian Ure from being lassoed.

Far from being kidnapped, all the students wanted to do was to get a picture with him! Ure was given a Mexican sombrero to put on before being draped in a big Scottish flag for the photo. He was told to take the flag with him and fly it from his hotel room when they got to Italy.

Ure and the Lion Rampant and Cox and his Magic Lamp flew out with the travelling party from

Edinburgh to London at 2.20pm on the next stage of the journey.

On arrival in London, the Dundee party almost bumped into Real Madrid who were on their way to play in Stoke City's centenary celebration match. As Dundee went in one door the Spanish champions came out another. One autograph hunter managed to get Alfredo Di Stefano and Bobby Seith to sign the same pad!

Boxer Brian London was sporting two black eyes in the terminal and found himself the centre of attention for photographers. 'If I had more time I'd fix up three rounds with him,' quipped Bert 'Punchy' Slater. London had just returned from Stockholm from a non-title 12-round match against Ingemar Johansson, which he lost on points.

Legendary boxing commentator Harry Carpenter spoke after the fight about the time he spent in Dundee at the start of World War Two. His fledgling career as a journalist was put on hold when he served in the Royal Navy as a Morse code operator and as a telegrapher in destroyers for the rest of the hostilities. He stayed in a hotel during the week while in Dundee then with the Scott family at weekends

'One of my main regrets is that I've never managed to maintain contact with the Scotts,' he said. 'When I returned to England I lost their address. Although I've been back in Dundee several times since the end of the war I've never had time to visit the places we used to haunt.'

Carpenter was the BBC's voice of boxing and covered his first Olympics in 1956 in Melbourne when he watched arguably Dundee's greatest-ever sportsman win boxing gold.

Dick McTaggart beat fighters from Sri Lanka, France and the Soviet Union on points to meet Harry Kurschat of the United Team of Germany in the Olympic lightweight final. The Dundonian defeated the European champion on points and that, along with his knockout achievements, put his home city firmly on the pugilistic map. He was also rewarded with a trophy as the most stylish boxer of the Melbourne Games with Carpenter describing McTaggart as 'the greatest amateur I ever saw'.

The Dundee team had to wait over an hour in London before boarding a Caravelle jet and flying over the Alps to arrive in Bergamo. Alex Stuart, Doug Houston and Ian Ure proudly held up their newly acquired Lion Rampant while passing through the arrivals gate.

The party was met by Milan officials at the airport including secretary Bruno Passalacqua. Bob Shankly was able to fix up training sessions at 10am and 2pm on Tuesday with a further session the following day.

Players and officials then got the bus to their hotel and arrived at 9pm after ten hours of travelling. Within minutes of checking in, Bobby Cox was told, 'Get a meal then go up to Lawrie Smith's room for treatment.' The defender was still limping and was reluctant to speak about his prospects of playing.

Scottish internationals Ure and Hamilton were sharing a room. They put up the Scotland flag to keep their promise to the students. Ure also managed to overcome the language barrier on Tuesday morning at breakfast. Coffee and rolls were on offer but Ure wanted honey instead of marmalade. He gave a demonstration of a bee in flight to the bemused Italian waiter but it was enough to ensure he got his honey on the table!

Autograph hunters in Bergamo were already making money from Dundee's star player following the team's arrival.

Some youngsters opened a market stall selling autographs of the Dundee team. Ure's signature was offered at the top price of 200 Lire.

Later, the Dundee players had a 90-minute workout including a seven-a-side game. Dundee practised their shooting. The Italian observers were particularly impressed by the performance of Andy Penman.

Cox didn't feel any pain immediately after the light morning workout with his team-mates but his knee soon began to ache and his heat treatment continued.

Shankly decided to cancel the training session scheduled for the afternoon and allowed 12 of the players, chairman James Gellatly and director Jack Swadel to do a spot of sightseeing by taking a bus trip to Lake Como. Ure and Cox stayed behind with Shankly and Kean.

Ure wanted to rest up and spent the afternoon relaxing in bed while Cox went to the ground of amateur side Ponte St Pietro at the Stadio Communale. There he was given the use of a therapeutic apparatus in a bid to ensure his presence in the starting line-up.

'Bobby can kick the ball without the slightest twinge but when he puts his full weight on his left leg or tries to twist and turn he feels it,' said Shankly. 'Under these circumstances I am very apprehensive about his chances of playing on Wednesday night.'

The Italian champions were training outside the city and Rocco named ten starters before listing Giuliano Fortunato, Paolo Barison and Gino Pivatelli for the outside-left position.

Mr Passalacqua said 70,000 tickets had already been sold and he was expecting a crowd of 80,000 because the world-renowned Milan Fair was also taking place in the city. He said many people from across the globe had decided to make the semi-final match their final fling before the trade fair closed the following day.

'We expect a very close result,' he said. 'I don't think either of the two games will produce many goals. Milan have scored only 45 in 30 league matches and we are a little worried about losing the scoring urge. We expect Dundee to have a solid defence. We will just have to break it down because we must get at least a two-goal lead for our trip to Scotland.'

Milan boss Nereo Rocco broke it down further.

'We prefer a defensive game with attacks in the form of sudden raids,' he said. 'It is not favourable to us to attack as a policy. Much would depend on the form of centre-forward José Altafini. This year he has been below form, but he will probably hit a goal-scoring patch one of these days. I hope it is tomorrow.'

The match would be refereed by Vicente Caballero from Spain, who had taken charge of the European Cup tie between Rangers and Standard Liege the previous season.

Shankly was confident of taking something from the game despite the standard of opposition. He said, 'I do not think we shall lose. But if we do it will be by only a narrow margin.'

The Dundee players and officials visited the San Siro that Tuesday evening before going to bed and were delighted with the condition of the pitch despite some heavy rain. They found the heat in Milan difficult to cope with and were glad the match would be played in the evening.

The first leg would coincide with another huge match-up with a Tayside connection. The Queen's cousin, Princess Alexandra, would walk down the aisle at Westminster Abbey to marry Old Etonian Mr Angus Ogilvy.

Though born in London in 1928, Mr Ogilvy, whose family had served the Royal Family for generations, had spent much of his childhood at Cortachy Castle on his father's estate near Kirriemuir. A painting of Cortachy Castle was amongst the gifts from employees of the estate, while tradespeople and friends of Kirriemuir and District would be presenting either a piece of antique furniture or a silver coffee pot, with the decision being left to the couple.

Just as big a decision would soon have to be made some 800 miles away in Milan.

Bobby Cox thought he might still make it but the final call on his fitness would be made on Wednesday morning. His absence, if he were to miss out, would be an immense blow to Dundee's chances of holding Milan as he was a huge influence in a tight-knit defence.

Would the magic lamp give Cox his wish of a start against Milan?

Chapter 13

Flashbulbs and Flashpoints

'It was all so ridiculous to us and his
actions definitely unsettled the team.'

Gordon Smith

SADLY, THERE was to be no fairy-tale recovery for
Bobby Cox who finally lost his fitness battle and was
ruled out of the first leg.

Dundee cancelled a morning treatment session with
Shankly now concerned that the knee injury was much
worse than first thought.

'It might even be cartilage trouble,' he said. 'We
just don't know.'

It was a huge blow for the Dens skipper. Cox was
unlikely to make the return leg at Dens the following
week and would also miss the chance of playing for

Scotland. Shankly confirmed that Alex Stuart, who was being groomed as a left-half, would replace Cox in the number three jersey. The tall Aberdonian had stepped in at half-back on three occasions during the championship season but his last appearance at left-back had been back in September 1960 when he played in the Dundee derby.

Doug Houston, who had just turned 20, would continue instead of the injured Hugh Robertson on the left wing. Bobby Seith would assume the captaincy and he predicted the team would thrive in front of a full house at the San Siro.

He said, 'After our great win over Anderlecht in Belgium I was asked how we could go such a long way and win 4-1 against a team that had beaten Real Madrid, then flop dismally three days later at Airdrie. We played in front of 60,000 in Belgium, where the tension was red-hot. At Broomfield there were 4,000 and the atmosphere was as cold as last month's weather.

'Only against teams like Rangers, Celtic and Hearts – and of course in local derbies – in Scotland can you arouse the atmosphere of our two games against Anderlecht. Every week in England you play in front of something like 20,000. If Dundee played before crowds like that every week we'd be an even greater side.'

The Dundee players spent the afternoon in bed following a final training session at San Pietro before leaving the hotel in Bergamo at 7pm to make the journey to the San Siro. The kick-off was delayed by 13 minutes to allow the 78,000 fans to get inside. They first watched a game between two Milan junior sides aged between 11 and 15.

Among the spectators was a deputation from defending champions Benfica. They had achieved a scoreless draw in the first leg of their semi-final against Feyenoord but, in the expectation that they would overcome the Dutch in the Lisbon return, were there to do their homework on their prospective opponents.

There was also a galaxy of officials from other foreign clubs and a tremendous gathering of journalists and media from across Europe, with even those from the Eastern bloc taking an interest.

Among the fans in the Dundee end was master baker Thomas Donaldson Duncan, who made a four and a half hour train journey from Switzerland where he was with a party of Scottish bakers.

Also in the crowd were three RAF boys who were stationed at Malta. They flew over to Sicily before hitch-hiking all the way north to Milan. They had been sleeping in the open and surviving on sandwiches and whisky.

In the event, Dundee would also be left feeding off scraps. Milan it appeared had gone for an attacking formation with the towering Barison on the left wing.

AC Milan: Ghezzi, David, Trebbi, Benitez, Maldini, Trapattoni, Mora, Sani, Altafini, Rivera, Barison.

Dundee: Slater, Hamilton, Stuart, Seith, Ure, Wishart, Smith, Penman, Cousin, Gilzean, Houston.

In the opening minutes, Alex Stuart made a last-gasp tackle on Altafini when the forward was clean through following a pass from Rivera.

But the quick goal Milan were after – and which Dundee were desperate to avoid – came after just three minutes.

Gordon Smith was judged to have fouled Barison on the byline. When the winger sailed the free kick into the packed goalmouth, Sani headed the ball into the far corner of the net.

Dundee picked themselves up from the early disappointment. A move between Seith and Penman put Cousin through but he was pulled back for offside. Another free kick was then given against Gordon Smith for alleged handling and this time Altafini headed narrowly past.

The home crowd whistled and booed Dundee's every touch. They weren't the only ones eager to whistle. The away side's cause wasn't helped by the Spanish referee Caballero, whose performance in the early stages was already raising a few eyebrows.

Caballero awarded 15 free kicks against Dundee in the first 15 minutes and appeared to be pulling back their players for any tackles that they made. The Dark Blues, on the other hand, were being subjected to some tough tackling which was going unpunished. Smith and Gilzean in particular were singled out.

Tommy Gallacher, writing for *The Courier*, said the referee's whistle had never been silent during the opening exchanges and 'Milan were being given everything'. He said, 'some of the referee's decisions were ridiculous.'

The absence of both Cox and Robertson made Dundee's left flank a prime target. Rocco sought to exploit this by switching Altafini out to the right, where he kept Alex Stuart on his toes from the off. The 22-year-old was relatively inexperienced but any fears that he would be out of his depth proved unfounded and he was giving a good account of himself, despite what was being thrown at him.

Milan were going all out for goals and battering the Dundee backline, where Bert Slater was constantly in action, though Dundee's counter-attacking had started to provide a few chances.

Alan Cousin scored on 22 minutes when Andy Penman broke through on the right with a fine run and provided the perfect cross for his team-mate to head home. Three minutes later, a Smith cross looked promising for Gilzean but he was given offside as he was challenged by two Milan defenders.

Play shifted quickly to the other end and Slater saved desperately at Barison's feet. High crosses were causing most of the problems for Dundee. Alex Hamilton injured his leg in a tackle on winger Paolo Barison shortly afterwards, which served to further weigh down Dundee's ability to defend the flanks.

Rivera almost caught Slater napping when he slipped a low one to the near post instead of the customary high lob. Dundee could have gone behind when Sani sent in a point-blank header only for Slater to save at the second attempt.

The game was becoming a succession of lobs into the Dundee goalmouth, interspersed with free kicks, all for Milan, and all for mysterious reasons. On 33 minutes, from another of these free kicks awarded by Caballero, given against Alex Stuart, Altafini's header scraped the top of the bar.

The Dens men might have gone in ahead at the break but Gilzean failed to connect with a cross from Houston. The Dark Blues, then, went in level, and Shankly called for more of the same in the second half.

The manager also made a complaint to the match officials because Slater was being blinded by a battery of camera flashes every time he went for the ball. There were 15 Italian press photographers who had gathered behind Slater's goal and it appeared as if they were all flashing their bulbs at the same time. Only three photographers were situated behind the home goal.

The Dundee goalkeeper moaned that he had been blinded several times but Shankly's protest to referee Caballero and the Italian officials was to no avail.

In contrast to the Dundee message of 'more of the same', Milan received the hairdryer treatment from Rocco and looked a different side when they came back out of the tunnel.

Dundee fell behind in controversial fashion after the restart when Victor Benitez appeared to cross from behind the line but the linesman didn't flag. Barison outjumped Ure and Hamilton to flight a glorious header out of Slater's reach and into the far corner.

Now only a series of fine saves from Slater kept Milan at bay, but soon the defence was overwhelmed.

Stuart brought down Benitez with a flying tackle on 53 minutes. A ball was floated into the penalty area and Altafini was the only man to jump. His header struck the inside of the crossbar and came down off Slater. There was Mora to prod home.

Dundee appealed for an infringement because Altafini, who was standing close to the post on the goal line, looked offside. In those days there was no grey area over the offside rule. Offside was offside. But there could be little argument that Altafini wasn't interfering with play when he lifted up his foot to allow Mora's shot to go underneath it.

Dundee protested and at one point it looked like the referee was indicating offside. But the linesman ran away from the Dundee protests and into the six-yard area, waving his flag furiously, and pointed towards the centre circle.

The goal was given.

Dundee were 3-1 down but almost pulled back the deficit when the impressive Doug Houston charged his way through the Italian backline.

The youngster ought to have gone round Ghezzi but with his legs feeling like rubber after his lung-bursting run, he thought he might run out of steam and instead struck a weak shot at the keeper, who had narrowed the angle.

Dundee were bewildered by Caballero's interpretation of the rules after he whistled them up for practically every tackle with bodily contact.

Another fright for Dundee came when Mora, now on the other side, burst through by beating Hamilton and cutting in. Slater palmed down his effort and pounced on the ball at the second attempt.

Dundee were struggling to get forward and the home side looked content to sit back before going further in front on 77 minutes. A curling cross eluded

Slater's fingertips and Barison rose above the struggling Hamilton at the near post to head home.

Milan went looking for more goals. Altafini should have scored but Slater blocked and saved.

With eight minutes left, Mora put Milan 5-1 up with his head and effectively extinguished Dundee's Wembley hopes. Towards the end, Cousin and Penman broke through but Cousin's shot shook the crossbar to prove that it was just not Dundee's night.

The dice appeared to be heavily loaded against Dundee from the off.

All the Milan goals had come off the back of high crosses against the backdrop of a wall of light from the Italian press photographers. The Italians had 12 corners to Dundee's one. During the game Dundee were penalised by 29 free kicks to Milan's tally of 15. Tommy Gallacher said the referee showed such bias that every time a Dundee player went near their Italian counterparts, he made it impossible for them to tackle.

Dundee were incensed about the referee's attitude and some of the players suggested that it was all too obvious whose side he was on.

Cousin said, 'There were several factors that seemed to go against us. We certainly got no breaks at all. I had equalised with a header and it was 1-1 at half-time. But after the break Milan scored two goals that were the result of dubious refereeing decisions. There was also talk about a volley of flashbulbs being discharged around our goalmouth. All their goals came from high crosses and there was the suspicion that our defenders, normally very good in the air, were being blinded.'

Winger Gordon Smith didn't hold back. He said, 'I have seen many bad referees in my time but this time was easily the worst. It reached the point where we were not allowed even to put in a foot to try and take the ball away from the Milan players. It was all so ridiculous to us and his actions definitely unsettled the team.

'Some of the lads think Milan are a better side than any we have met but I would put them behind Cologne and Anderlecht. The Italians scored two quick goals early in the second half and after that were able to play well with everything going their way. I feel we could have come home with two goals less to make up.'

Smith also took aim at the domestic football authorities for failing to ease the fixture congestion by not giving Dundee more time to prepare for the match.

'As far as I can see they've done nothing at all,' he said. 'We had a very strenuous game in the mud and water against Dundee United in midweek and I felt we should have been excused playing last Saturday.'

Shankly was also extremely unhappy at the officiating but admitted that his own team's failings had also contributed to the outcome.

He said, 'Despite the referee, I must say the team did not play too well. Milan are a good side with several clever individuals. When the score was 1-1, I had the feeling we had them worried but it was all over after they scored two quick goals.'

Former referee Tommy Small blasted Caballero's performance after the match and praised the Dundee players for allowing the Spanish whistler to leave the pitch in one piece.

'I've never seen anything like him in all my experience,' he said. 'I feel I must commend the Dundee team for showing great restraint. I am sure if it had been a foreign side getting that kind of treatment somebody would have floored the referee.'

Ure also blasted the official and confirmed he had not allowed Dundee to tackle. He felt that he had 'played a stinker', but the big centre-half had still impressed the Italians.

Rocco's right-hand man Gipo Viani said Penman was Dundee's best player with Ure a close second, while goalkeeper Ghezzi described Ure as 'so strong and fearless'. He thought Milan or Roma would have no hesitation in paying £150,000 for the Scotland international.

The Dundee players and officials attended the after-match banquet in the Continentale Hotel which was attended by José Crahay from UEFA. Caballero had been given strict instructions to be tough and Crahay congratulated him on his firm control, but Dens chairman James Gellatly was less than impressed.

He said, 'We have been fortunate with refs so far. Something like this was bound to happen.'

Ian Ure and Gordon Smith were great admirers of the Italian game and Milan in particular but the feeling was to grow that Dundee had been hard done by.

At the banquet Dundee players were presented with watches inscribed AC Milan which were enclosed in a miniature car tyre. The club received a silver salver.

The Dundee party returned to their hotel in Bergamo at 4am but didn't get much sleep. Three hours later they were ready to start the homeward journey and left at 8am for the airport.

The Italian papers in the lobby didn't give Dundee any chance of overturning the deficit in the second leg. As far as they were concerned it would be Milan, who had now scored 33 goals and conceded six in the competition, against Benfica in the final.

The Italian sports journalists believed that if Dundee's second-half tactics had been different they might have got a result.

The *Corriere della Sera* said, 'Never in this year's national championship did Milan appear so overwhelming.' The article suggested the Italians could face the return match with 'tranquillity' given they were going to Dens with a four-goal advantage.

La Gazetta dello Sport said the outcome of the first leg had been uncertain until Milan scored the third goal on 53 minutes.

Il Giorno said five of the goals were headed in and gave the explanation that the floodlights were able to dazzle goalkeeper Bert Slater because he was not tall. The paper praised the performances of Ure and Penman despite the result.

Dundee flew back to London at 10.15am and had to wait three hours before catching another plane to Turnhouse.

Alex Hamilton had joined Bobby Cox on the injury list after taking a knock at the San Siro. Cox had bowed to the inevitable and faced a cartilage operation.

'I want to get this over as quickly as possible,' he said. 'As far as I'm concerned this season finished last Saturday. Now I want to get fit for the next.'

He revealed that he had first felt his knee in the cup replay against Rangers and admitted to being a 'wee bit disappointed' at missing the chance to play for Scotland 'though that's how it goes and I'm not going to mope about it'.

The defender did have one further complaint, and it wasn't his knee. He had to visit the dentist for toothache.

Chapter 14

Singing the Blues

'That is what is wrong with some Scottish
players – too much whisky!'

Gipo Viani, AC Milan

DINO SANI had also been injured and was doubtful for the return leg in Dundee. The Brazilian star was to have extensive treatment in the days ahead but had already been ruled out of Milan's league game that Sunday against Genoa.

Sani would take medical advice and go with the flow. A similar picture was occurring in Dundee, where a 30-foot fountain of water burst out in the middle of the Nethergate.

The first phase of the Overgate redevelopment scheme was nearing completion when the drama unfolded. An excavator was levelling the ground when the machine shovel knocked the top off a pipe valve and water went shooting into the air. After reaching its full height the water cascaded 50 yards down Nethergate and passers-by dashed for safety in shop doors as the water lashed at their feet.

Dundee suffered their own deluge of goals in Milan. Now they returned to domestic fare with a visit from a Raith Rovers side rooted to the foot of the league.

There was no Hamilton and Cox and home fans were faced with an unfamiliar full-back pairing of Shug Reid alongside his erstwhile reserve-team partner Alex Stuart.

Raith fans had been delayed due to a train derailment which caused the main Aberdeen–Edinburgh line to be blocked for three hours just outside Kirkcaldy. A train of wagons loaded with coal from the Seafield Colliery came off the tracks around 8.50am.

Trains from both directions were unable to get through and eight double-decker buses were used to shuttle 1,200 to 1,500 passengers between Dundee and Kirkcaldy. Around 12 trains were held up before the line was cleared at noon.

Dundee, who rested Gordon Smith, similarly ran out of steam in a disappointing 1-1 draw. Understandably, the players had one eye on the return leg of their European Cup semi-final but even so it was hardly the best of encouragement for what was sure to be an all or nothing effort against the Italians.

Milan, meanwhile, rested six players – Sani, Rivera, David, Maldini, Benitez and Barison – and won 1-0 against Genoa. Altafini was always a source of danger and he scored the winning goal on 69 minutes.

The Milan players were said to be on a highly lucrative £700 a man to reach the European Cup Final and would fly out to Dundee on Monday.

Frankie Vaughan, whose singing career started in the late 1940s, was also getting ready to travel to Dundee after he finally found a place to sing.

In 1955 he recorded the song 'Give Me The Moonlight' that became his trademark and theme, and which he generally sang at the end of his stage act. The legendary crooner's visit to the city would fulfil an ambition of Murdo Wallace Jr, the son of the famous Dundee ballroom proprietor.

Since he was 14, Murdoch had wanted to organise and present an established star in the city and the chance arrived when he visited an agent friend in Glasgow. During the conversation, he was told that Vaughan had one date free in his tightly packed schedule.

The agent suggested he invite the star for a one-night stand in Scotland. Murdoch jumped at the chance, took up the available date and managed to book Green's Playhouse for the show on 5 May.

AC Milan were without Dino Sani, who failed to recover from his injury, when they arrived at Turnhouse Airport from London to be greeted by Bob Shankly and other Dundee officials.

Manager Nereo Rocco said it would be a 'very hard and difficult match' but he thought his side had a big enough advantage to progress to the final.

'We shall try for a draw but I'm sure we'll face an unleashed team out to win the match, if not to qualify for the final,' he said.

'Barring unforeseen events, the team will be the same as in the first match, except for Sani, who will be replaced by Gino Pivatelli.'

Goalkeeper Ghezzi hinted that AC Milan were unlikely to go on the offensive at Dens Park.

'Everybody will come back to me,' he said. 'But if we lose goals then we must change our plans.'

There was better news regarding Dundee right-back Alex Hamilton. He had trained but didn't take part in the practice match with the rest of the players.

'Hammy' instead contented himself by standing behind the goal where he kicked a few balls into the net. The Scotland international seemed happy with the way his leg stood up and Shankly said he was almost certain to play. Alex Stuart took part in the practice game at left-back and would play there again against Milan. Interestingly, reserve centre-half George Ryden was utilised at inside-right but any thoughts of a Shankly master plan would prove far-fetched!

Bobby Cox was also at Dens watching his team-mates before being put in a wheelchair to go into a nursing home for his cartilage operation. He would be in good company as reserve full-back Norrie Beattie was to undergo the same procedure.

Cox still believed the team could make the final. He said, 'I think the boys are in with a chance. If they can get two goals in the first half I think they'll pull through. After all, four of Milan's goals came in the second half.

'Dundee will have a strong support, I don't think we will make as many mistakes this time and the refereeing cannot possibly be as bad. I know four goals are a lot but Cologne pulled back four goals on us in Germany, and might have got more if they had kept their heads.

'I don't think our task is impossible and nor do any of the players. My only regret is that I won't be able to play myself but I'll be rooting for the boys knowing that if they get the breaks they have the ability to reach the final.'

The Milan party travelled north in two coaches and arrived at the Royal Hotel in Dundee at 7.45pm. An Italian waiter ensured there were no language difficulties and in next to no time they were tucking into huge steaks.

Assistant manager Gipo Viani said Milan insisted on a special diet for their players.

'Yes, very much so,' he said. 'Soup, meat, steaks and more steaks, mineral water, vegetables, rice and lots of fruit. Some wine but no whisky. That is what is wrong with some Scottish players – too much whisky!' he joked.

He said they were 'very, very surprised' to read negative comments about the performance of referee Vicente Caballero in the British press.

'We have no complaints,' Viani said. When asked about the repeated camera flashes from behind the Dundee goal which upset Bert Slater, Viani said, 'It was not too bad. The goals were scored by the head. Slater was out of position. The cameras had nothing to do with it. Perhaps it may have made him nervous though.'

He said it was 'possible' they would try to buy Pelé if they won the European Cup but also said he liked Ian Ure, who he described as a modern defender.

The Courier's Tommy Gallacher managed to pin down Rocco for a chat.

'Through the helpful services of Alex, an Italian waiter, who acted as an interpreter' the journalist was quick to discover similarities between the Italian boss and Shankly: 'No messing about and to the point!'

Gallacher asked him if he thought that Caballero had been too harsh on Dundee's tackling in Milan?

Rocco replied, 'I don't think so at all. Surely the Scots are not blaming the 5-1 defeat on the referee? Referees are the same the whole world over. There is only one on the field but there are 22 players.'

The Courier man also asked him how he would set out his team for the second leg.

Rocco said, 'We will play defensively if we have to. And we will attack if we have to. In the first leg we had to get goals with the return in mind. But Dundee forced us to play the way we did by back-pedalling into their penalty area.

'I saw Dundee play Anderlecht in Brussels and they played the same game.

'And it wasn't until they were leading 3-1 that they really went on the attack.'

Would there be any special tactics?

'No, no,' said Rocco. 'Football is a simple game. Too many ideas only complicate it. Dundee played much better in Brussels than in Milan. I think they will be hard to beat. I don't mind if Dundee win 2-1, 3-1, or even 4-1, as long as they don't win 4-0!'

There was concern the first-leg result would make many fans decide to stay away, unlike the situation as the Old Firm prepared to go to war the following Saturday.

More than 100 forged tickets for the 130,000 sell-out Scottish Cup Final between Rangers and Celtic had just been handed in to police. It emerged that they had been bought by fans in pubs and betting shops.

Chief Constable James Robertson warned fans that officers would be able to tell which tickets were forged and which were the genuine article. Special police would be on operation at that game and fans were also being urged to be on their guard against strangers trying to sell them tickets for the match.

On Tuesday, the Milan players had a long lie-in then a light breakfast of coffee and rolls before doing a spot of shopping in the city. High on their list was the world famous Scotch whisky and the group returned to the Royal Hotel with over 20 bottles between them.

Most of the players also bought postcards to send back home to Italy. A popular card was one of a boy in a kilt crying his eyes out with the caption: 'Greetin's frae Dundee'.

The Italian players were feeling the cold and goalkeeper Giorgio Ghezzi was still shivering despite being dressed in a thick overcoat.

'I thought it was nearly summer here too,' he said. 'We don't need coats in Milan just now.'

The Italians were invited for coffee with the Lord Provost at the City Chambers at noon and would get their first look at Dens where they had a training session set up for 7.30pm. Lord Provost McManus wished the visitors the very happiest stay in the city with one exception – they were not to win tomorrow night's match.

Milan player Luigi Radice said the Italian party was very happy to be in Dundee. He said the city was well known to him for its historical background and its industrial importance. He said all Italians remembered the English and Scots for their leadership in the fight for liberty during the Second World War. As to the match, he said he hoped the crowd would see a very good game with the best team winning.

Milan were later taken on a bus tour of the city and the team spent the rest of the day relaxing before heading to Dens for training.

Many years before it was seriously considered in the British game – Gordon Smith apart – it was clear that the visitors took their diet very seriously. Their club doctor had already made one change to their original meal chart and the players' pre-match meal included rice, which they brought with them from Italy.

Referee Lucien van Nuffell and his linesmen were met at the station by Shankly and Dundee director Robert Crichton at 11pm that night. The following day the three Belgian officials went shopping for tartan souvenirs before the now-traditional tour of the Keiller's factory provided by John Gordon.

The Milan players spent the day of the match relaxing in the hotel or looking around town and were to come across a future singing star when they went for a walk in the Nethergate. Gianni Rivera was among those who shook hands with an 11-year-old boy who would go on to achieve stardom in his own right as the 'Bard of Dundee'. Michael Marra, who would become one of Scotland's most respected singer-songwriters, recalled years later that he thought the Milan players looked like film stars.

He wasn't the only one. Dundee had never experienced excitement like it. Dundee chairman James Gellatly was just as blown away by it all.

He said the European Cup had been a 'memorable experience' for the club. 'To reach the semi-final we had to account for Cologne, Sporting Lisbon and Anderlecht, all of whom are among the top clubs in Europe. It is gratifying that, thanks to the spirit and ability of the team, we have been able to confound the critics and put the city of Dundee on the international football map.

'As we progressed from round to round our supporters began to appreciate that our team was worthy of support, with the result that by the time we played Anderlecht, the attendance had increased from 24,500 at the first match, to almost 40,000.

'It is a very expensive business for Scottish clubs to compete against the continental clubs with resources based on attendances of 60–70,000 supporters at much higher prices, as we do not participate in the away gates, but are dependent on our home support which in the case of Dundee is limited to a maximum of 40,000.'

Mr Gellatly said Dundee had been the 'unknown team in the competition' and were given little chance of surviving the preliminary round. He said the encouragement from the fans had contributed in no small measure to their success and they could not have survived the challenges from Germany, Portugal and Belgium without it.

'I would say a special word of appreciation to the not inconsiderable number of fans who have travelled to all our away matches,' he said. 'Even they can hardly realise the wonderful uplift which it gives to the team when playing before a crowd of perhaps 60,000 to hear the vociferous support of several hundred unmistakably Dundee voices.'

As in the previous rounds, the *Evening Telegraph* published a magnificent European Cup souvenir programme and these were to be found on the counters and in the windows of newsagents and other retail outlets throughout the city and beyond.

Fernando Caiado, assistant coach and technical secretary of Benfica, was in the Dens Park stand to watch his team's European Cup Final opponents. The former Benfica midfielder had been capped 16 times for Portugal and played against Scotland in 1955.

He then turned to coaching, temporarily stepping in as manager at the end of the 1961/62 season following the departure of Bela Guttmann, the Holocaust survivor who rose from the death pits of Europe to become a legendary figure at the Lisbon club.

Caiado said Benfica were confident of disposing of Feyenoord in Lisbon the following Wednesday to make the final at Wembley but wrote off Dundee's chances of pulling off a miracle.

He had watched the Dark Blues against Sporting Lisbon but said the four-goal deficit would be too much to pull back against one of the best sides on the continent. The Dark Blues' chances of becoming the first British team in the final did appear remote.

It was now 1 May and a bright but blowy summer evening in Dundee as the teams lined up:

Dundee: Slater, Hamilton, Stuart, Seith, Ure, Wishart; Smith, Penman, Cousin, Gilzean, Houston.

AC Milan: Ghezzi, David, Radice, Benitez, Maldini, Trapattoni, Mora, Pivatelli, Altafini, Rivera, Barison.

Hugh Robertson had returned for the visit of Raith Rovers but Doug Houston was back in the team for Dundee's last throw of the dice against the Italian maestros.

Nearly 37,000 fans were on the Dens Park slopes as Dundee looked to leave nothing in the dressing room and went for goals straight from the kick-off.

They might have had a penalty on three minutes when Gilzean was pushed off the ball going for a Smith free kick in the Milan goalmouth. On eight minutes Pivatelli appeared to handle a Seith shot but another penalty appeal was turned down.

The Italians were set up to keep things tight and hit Dundee on the break. Altafini almost put the contest out of sight after ten minutes when he pulled down a high ball and beat Seith and Ure in quick succession.

A goal seemed certain but Slater came out to narrow the angle and the Italian side-footed the ball inches past the post.

On 14 minutes, Seith almost opened the scoring for Dundee. He gathered a pass from Hamilton and struck from 22 yards. Ghezzi tipped his shot over the bar.

With 20 minutes played, tempers flared when Benitez was left writhing in agony following a Gilzean tackle which took the referee a few minutes to sort out. There was plenty of needle and both teams were fighting tooth and nail.

The Italian champions were impressive at the back, no surprise given manager Rocco was the master of the Catenaccio system. Nominally at inside-right, Pivatelli played as the libero behind the centre-backs to recover loose balls and help lead the counter-attack.

Dundee could have been awarded yet another spot kick near the half-hour mark. Ghezzi gathered the ball before Gordon Smith was unceremoniously thrown to the ground by Peruvian international Benitez some eight yards away.

A few minutes later, Dundee's luck was out again when Alan Gilzean appeared to have been deliberately fouled inside the box as he ran in to meet a cross. On both occasions the Belgian referee awarded free kicks for obstruction.

A mix-up between David and Maldini gave Penman a chance on goal but Ghezzi dived at his feet before he could shoot. In the isolated Milan attacks, Ure was looking unbeatable for Dundee.

Things finally looked up just a minute before the break. A twice-taken free kick from the left was headed clear and picked up by Smith. The veteran playmaker quickly chipped the ball into the middle with his left foot and Alan Gilzean rose to head home and give Dundee the opener.

At half-time a young fan transferred his big lucky horseshoe from one net to the other. Still three behind on aggregate, Dundee needed all the help they could get.

Dundee fans started to dream when they scored again within a minute of the restart. Penman put the ball in the net from a Gilzean knock-down. But the hope was short-lived as Gilzean was judged to have been offside when he got his head to the ball despite the linesman having flagged for a goal.

'I had blown my whistle for offside on Gilzean before Penman hit his shot,' said the referee.

Dundee kept up the attack and Ghezzi had to punch out desperately to foil Gilzean after Wishart took a free kick from the edge of the box.

Dundee kept fighting but were now looking for a miracle and Milan almost equalised when Gianni Rivera went on a quick run through the middle. The 19-year-old couldn't finish it off and Bert Slater pushed his shot past for a corner.

The Italians now threw off their defensive blanket and started to attack. Mora picked up a free kick and ran forward before taking a shot which struck Ure and went past the post.

Dundee should have scored midway through the second half when Alan Cousin broke through on the left and passed to Gilzean, who was in space. Gilzean's shot was blocked and Penman blazed the ball wildly over from the rebound.

Milan used every trick in the book to make sure the miracle comeback didn't happen. The Dark Blues flooded forward but were often stopped by a kick or a punch. Smith complained he was being fouled every time he was on the ball. Gilzean was also targeted and afforded similar rough treatment while the man in the middle from Belgium had a tough job to ensure tempers didn't boil over. Dundee's opponents were also guilty of play-acting and time-wasting to burn down the clock. This time Milan were penalised for 29 fouls to Dundee's 17.

Alex Stuart was making some excellent tackles at left-back but, with 15 minutes remaining, Slater almost gave Milan the equaliser when he completely misjudged a Barison cross.

Mora picked up the ball on the byline only for his soft effort to hit the side of the post. The goalie recovered to turn a Rivera shot round the post two minutes later.

Dundee were still fighting hard but struggling to create and their own goal was being put under serious pressure.

The home side went down to ten men with eight minutes to go. Gilzean was ordered off after finally losing his temper and lashing out at his marker Benitez. There was little excuse for his behaviour, although it was hard not to have sympathy with Dundee's top scorer, who had spent almost the entire match being kicked.

There was no further scoring and, despite their massive disappointment at failing to reach the

European Cup Final, Dundee sportingly lined up to applaud Milan off the field.

Though defeated, Dundee had every right to be proud of their own performance. The fighting spirit shown by the team was also hugely appreciated by the supporters. They had remained unbeaten at home during their European escapades, no mean feat given the standard of opposition over the four rounds.

Gordon Smith said the refereeing was 100% better at Dens.

He said, 'If only we had scored two goals in the first half, or even if we had got that Penman counter early in the second, we might have done it. The fans can't say we didn't try.'

Alex Hamilton said, 'If we had had that referee in Milan it would have been a different story.'

From the start, the Italians had looked to break up play by fair means or foul. Van Nuffell had handled a difficult game and had certainly been much fairer than his Spanish counterpart in Milan, though he had still managed to turn down at least two penalty appeals and chalked off a goal for offside.

Alex Stuart's performance was one of the highlights for Dundee but, although many rated him the outstanding defender, much of the post-match attention again focused on his team-mate Ian Ure.

Even Van Nuffell joined in the praise. He said, 'This was my 58th match involving sides from different countries. It was a very hard and difficult match for me. But all through there was one gentleman and a magnificent player – Ure. Ure is the best centre-half I've seen in 30 years as a referee.

'I was sorry to order off Gilzean but I had no choice. You must remember the television cameras were showing this match all over Europe, and if I had not ordered off Gilzean I would have been ordered off.'

Stand-in captain Seith said, 'We fought hard and we are consoling ourselves with the fact that we at least did win, so our record in the European Cup is won five, lost three, which is pretty good.

'I thought Penman's scoring shot should have been allowed in the second half, and we should have had those penalties in the first period. But our biggest stumbling block was the four-goal margin. If it had just been a couple I think we could have pulled it off.'

Benfica's technical secretary Fernando Caiado was already planning for Wembley and Dundee's players would be able to watch the outcome of the second leg of the other semi-final, which was to be televised live on the Eurovision link the following week.

Caiado suggested Ure would soon be lighting up television screens across Europe from an altogether bigger stage than he was currently performing on. 'Dundee's centre-half must find a place in a bigger club,' he said. 'He's got everything to be a world-class footballer. I thought Milan were happy to let Dundee come to them. We can expect a different team in the final.'

Shankly believed the Dark Blues might have been able to run Milan close if they'd got a quick goal. He said, 'I thought the boys played hard, and we should have had at least two penalties.'

The Dens boss was also quizzed about Ure, who was now being linked with a move to Arsenal.

'There has been no approach by Arsenal for his transfer,' said Shankly. 'I read stories that Ure is wanting away but as yet I've not spoken to him about the terms the club has offered for next season.'

Dundee, he said, would be retaining all their 28 players.

At the post-match banquet, Dundee chairman James Gellatly said his team had fully justified their position as Scottish champions by giving the fans a wonderful show in the European Cup.

For his part, Nereo Rocco said Dundee played much better in the second leg and praised the performances of Hamilton, Stuart, Ure and Penman – with a special word for Stuart who he described as a 'magnificent deputy'.

While there, Milan officials inquired about Ure, saying they would pay £60,000 if he became available. However, Dundee made it clear they wanted their prize asset to stay put and suggested that any offer should be made in writing.

That same night, Tottenham Hotspur and Jimmy Greaves booked their place in the European Cup Winners' Cup Final with a 3-1 win against OFK Belgrade. It was a deserved achievement but one which Dundee fans could only observe with a degree of envy.

Bobby Cox had just managed to stay awake long enough to see the highlights on television. He had gone under the knife in hospital and was still drowsy from the anaesthetic following his cartilage operation. The Dens skipper described Milan captain Cesare Maldini as 'something special' and 'probably the best centre-half I've ever seen'.

His operation was a complete success and he would recover in a private room in a Dundee nursing home. Cox, who was a keen golfer, was also told by Shankly to keep the clubs locked up during the summer until he was able to play football again.

He was given the match ball from the second leg by his team-mates. It was put alongside the match ball which was used when he skippered the team to the league title in Perth in 1962 and the other from his fortuitous raffle win after the 4-1 Anderlecht triumph in Brussels.

Chapter 15

Absent Friends

*'Dundee would have been European
champions if we'd got to the final, because
nobody would have beaten us at Wembley.'*

Craig Brown

'THE BATTLE'S O'er!' read the headline in that Friday's *People's Journal*.

It was a fitting epitaph to the Dark Blues' European Cup campaign on a weekend when both Frankie Vaughan and Dundee could be said to be singing the blues. The Dundee-based periodical gave its take on Wednesday's night's match at Dens.

'"Scythe 'em down, shake hands and we're all pals in sport," seemed to be the Milan motto in their determination to hold onto their four-goal lead.

'Thirty-seven thousand fans hadn't seen the likes before at Dens Park and this could be said of their team's performance in their progress to this last bitter battle.

'This match apart, Dundee had given the fans something to remember in the European Cup. They had taken on the champions of Germany, Portugal, Belgium and Italy and beaten the lot.

'But it was apparent from the game in Milan and on Wednesday night that there's more than ability needed to play the game well in this competition – a good and fair referee is a must.

'Body-checking, jersey-pulling and elbowing all bring down the wrath of a Scots referee but their continental counterparts never seem to have heard of ungentlemanly conduct.

'At least Dundee had the good grace to accept defeat in the traditions of British sport.

'But perhaps a little more devil and less turning the other cheek would be better.

'Anyway, Wednesday's match will be argued for many a day. It was a memorable occasion and we can thank Dundee for the memory of a wonderful page in the club's history.

'Cologne, Lisbon, Brussels, Milan. These names should be sewn on the league championship flag as glorious battle honours.'

Meanwhile, Benfica went on to defeat Feyenoord 3-1 before 74,000 fans in Lisbon to reach the final against Milan at Wembley on 22 May.

The Portuguese side had proven their quality by lifting the trophy in successive years but Milan had certainly made a statement in getting to Wembley by hitting 31 goals in eight games. It was the highest ratio in the competition's history at that time.

The towering Paolo Barison, an Italian international who had caused Dundee major problems out wide in the San Siro, and scorer of six goals in the competition, found himself dropped.

Instead, Milan fielded Gino Pivatelli, whose job was to shackle Benfica's left-half and playmaker, Mário Coluna.

It was a radical move, but one that was to pay rich dividends.

Eusébio put Benfica ahead after 18 minutes, but there was to be no third European Cup triumph in a row for the Red Eagles of Lisbon. The deadly Altafini struck twice for Milan. With Benfica skipper Coluna suffering a broken bone in his foot following a tackle by Pivatelli, the Rossoneri stood firm and saw out the game.

Benfica were so distraught that they almost forgot to collect their runners-up medals.

Unsurprisingly, Jimmy Greaves was at the match 'in his own manor', as he might have said. Just a week earlier, he had been a key man in Tottenham Hotspur's 5-1 European Cup Winners' Cup Final triumph against Atlético Madrid in Rotterdam. That made Bill Nicholson's side the first British club to win a major European trophy. Having seen his old club emulate that success, Greaves enjoyed a post-match Wembley reconciliation with his former protagonist, Milan boss Nereo Rocco.

There were several outstanding performers for Milan. Skipper Cesare Maldini, so highly thought of by Bobby Cox, was the man who lifted the trophy.

But of all the players faced by Dundee, left-half Giovanni Trapattoni was to have the most remarkable career. He was considered the most loyal and consistent disciple of Rocco's methods and would go on to become the most successful club coach in the history of Serie A.

Back home, the Dundee players and their supporters could only look on with a degree of envy and think of what might have been.

The apparent bias shown by the Spanish officials in Milan was a continuing source of anger, particularly when referee Caballero was later 'found to have accepted extravagant gifts from the Italian club prior to the game' and was 'subsequently banned on various other charges of bribery'.

What might have been had that game in the San Siro been played on a level playing field? And who would have emerged victorious if Dundee had gone on to meet Benfica in the final? Would the game even have been played at Wembley? There were suggestions it might have been switched to a 'neutral' country had either Ipswich or Dundee gone all the way since the London stadium was seen as a 'home' game for the British clubs.

Craig Brown, Dundee's reserve-team captain who went on to become Scotland international manager, later said, 'Dundee would have been European champions if we'd got to the final, because nobody would have beaten us at Wembley. That's what Shankly said!'

Was Bob Shankly naive in his assessment that it was unnecessary to 'study' any of their illustrious opponents and instead relying on 'tips' from helpful locals? The Barison aerial dominance was perhaps a case in point.

Coaches, as evidenced by Rocco, were becoming increasingly tactically aware in their approach. Dunfermline's Jock Stein and Willie Waddell of Kilmarnock were soon to the fore in seeking to learn from their continental peers.

Remarkably, Dundee had used just 13 players during their European Cup run, though 21 in all competitions. Ally Donaldson later made the observation that the club travelled with wafer-thin squads that did not include a reserve goalkeeper – a ploy that might have backfired badly had Bert Slater ever been a late call-off.

Back in Italy after the European Cup triumph, Milan were brought back down to earth with a thump when they played their last game of the Serie A season against bottom club Palermo. Before 15,000 fans they were 2-1 up and in little danger of defeat when things turned ugly.

Jumping over the wire net fencing in their hundreds, the Sicilians brought play to a halt and chased the referee into the pavilion in the 69th minute. They proceeded to set the advertising hoardings alight. Both teams left the field and extra police were called in to shepherd the crowd back on to the terracing. After 13 minutes order was finally restored and the game resumed.

Eventually Milan won 3-1, finishing in third place in the league, six points behind champions Inter Milan and two points behind second-placed Juventus.

Meanwhile, the domestic season continued until 25 May in Scotland after being extended due to the unprecedented fixture backlog following the Big Freeze. That meant a heavy schedule for most clubs across the country, with Dundee cramming four of their last six games into an eight-day stretch.

The Dark Blues completed their season with a credible no-score draw with new league champions Rangers before a crowd of 17,000 at Dens to finish a disappointing ninth in the table. Dundee's mediocre league form had been in stark contrast to the brilliance shown in the European Cup run.

However, the weather and subsequent fixture pile-up had meant them playing 22 league and cup games since restarting on 6 March. That entailed around two games per week over a 12-week period. It was a punishing programme, even tougher for those clubs without sufficient experienced back-up. Indeed, Partick Thistle claimed the fixture congestion had cost them the chance of the title after running neck and neck with Rangers and Kilmarnock in early winter.

The flurry of fixtures, however, had given Bob Shankly the opportunity to give a further taste of first-team football to fringe players like Alex Stuart, Craig Brown, George Ryden, Bobby Waddell, Kenny Cameron and Tommy Mackle.

It had been a memorable year for Dundee. That first league championship win, the month-long trip for the New York international tournament, then the incredible run to the European Cup semi-final. This had taken place against the seasonal backdrop of a glorious summer, then a normal autumn before the worst winter weather conditions in living memory.

Dundee's achievement was remarkable when considering the demographics. In 1962, the population of Dundee – then Scotland's third city – was 180,000. Cologne had 750,000, Lisbon and Brussels each 1.5 million, Milan 2.5 million.

Little wonder then, as Ian Ure liked to put it, that Dundee were seen as the 'wee team' that had spectacularly over-performed!

There was huge excitement amongst the footballing public in Dundee and beyond in this golden era. Dundee had gone no further than Hibs or Rangers in the European Cup yet there was the perception that the Dens men had made the biggest impact to date.

They had a potent mix of youth and experience, bags of skill and scoring potential, strength of character and big-name personalities. They had star quality and football fans from far and wide found themselves captivated by Dundee's exploits on the European stage.

For Dundee FC aficionados of that era, there were one or two unanswered questions.

Having reverted to the V-necked jersey for the Cologne game, the dark blue crew-necked set – only used half a dozen times – was consigned to history. In contrast, the crew-necked change outfit of white with blue trimmings continued in use until spring. Then, the club reverted to their white with blue collar version for the Scottish Cup matches against Rangers and the European Cup tie against Milan at Dens, finally utilising a fifth strip of white with thin, dark blue stripes in a 5-2 home win over Third Lanark.

There was another query over the players' stockings. In team photos, Gordon Smith and Alan Cousin were pictured with dark blue socks and large white turndowns while their team-mates displayed just a slim band of white having rolled up the white turndown.

To maintain uniformity of appearance, a frustrated Shankly finally intervened. He instructed the kit manufacturer to redesign the socks which were to be dark blue with only a slim band of white.

So much for the trivia, but what would become of this great Dundee team?

As in the summer of 1962, Dundee's top stars Alan Gilzean and Ian Ure held out on re-signing, as did right-back Alex Hamilton. Ure was already having his head turned by English-based Scotland team-mates about the riches on offer down south. He was a man in demand following his European Cup heroics. Hamilton and Gilzean were eventually persuaded to stay but Ure was determined to move and Dundee reluctantly accepted his transfer request.

Arsenal manager Billy Wright moved quickly. In August 1963, the London giants splashed out £62,500 to secure Ure and break the world record fee for a centre-half. The big defender remained at Highbury for six years before spending a couple of seasons at Manchester United. He had a short spell afterwards with St Mirren then a brief foray into the world of management with East Stirling.

Bobby Cox, meanwhile, recovered from his second cartilage operation only to fall flat on his face before the first home match of the 1963/64 season against Airdrie. The Dundee skipper led the team down the ramp with ball in hand only to slip and fall headlong on to the gravel track when turning towards the Provost Road end. One local newspaper described it as 'the only slip Bobby made all evening' as Dundee won the match 2-1!

There were to be goals galore throughout that 1963/64 campaign. Rejuvenated by younger players such as George Ryden, Alex Stuart, Bobby Waddell and Kenny Cameron, and without the distraction of European football, the Dark Blues mounted a credible championship challenge for much of the season.

They also went all the way to the 1964 Scottish Cup Final while racking up an astonishing 156 goals in all competitions, including the short-lived Summer Cup.

Dundee were spearheaded again by the deadly Alan Gilzean with 52 goals. He was supported by Andy Penman who scored 30, with Bobby Waddell and Kenny Cameron contributing a further 40 goals.

Alex Stuart soon became a driving force at left-half and his powerful shooting made him a firm favourite with the fans.

As promised by Bob Shankly, Ryden was given the opportunity to make the vacant centre-half position his own following the departure of Ure. This he did with a series of stirring performances to make sure that Ure's old berth became his permanent property as the Dark Blues returned to winning ways.

One of the key factors in Dundee's success was the camaraderie of the players on and off the field, with many having been at Dens Park for five years or more.

At one point, Pat Liney, Ian Ure, George Ryden, Hugh Robertson, Craig Brown, Tommy Mackle and Doug Houston all lived together in digs in the city.

Pat Liney summed it up. 'We were all great friends,' he said. 'We lived together, played football together and went to the dancing together!'

In those days, players would often be seen around the town with some to be found at the corner of Reform Street and High Street beneath the H. Samuel clock after training. Alex Hamilton was a star attraction with his white Jaguar car and was a regular attendee at the old Dundee baths along with team-mate Gilzean.

There was to be further harmony when Hamilton cut a record as leader of Hammy and the Hamsters. The pop group included Craig Brown, Kenny Cameron, Alex Stuart and Hugh Robertson. Their April release was entitled 'My Dreams Came True' but, despite their local appeal, the call from *Top of the Pops* was never forthcoming.

Nor did their dreams come true! There was to be no glory finale in the Scottish Cup Final.

Bert Slater played heroically in defying one of the great Ibrox forward lines with a string of incredible saves but fatal lapses in concentration saw Rangers break Dundee hearts with two late goals before 120,000 fans at Hampden to take the treble.

Despite the result, 1963/64 had been a great season and over 5,000 cheering fans welcomed Shankly's squad as they made their way to a reception at Dundee's City Chambers.

Ure's earlier departure was the beginning of the break-up of that great side. In January 1964 George McGeachie, who had earlier moved to Teesside to work for ICI, joined Fourth Division Darlington for £2,000. He played for another three seasons before his career was cut short by injury.

Championship hero Pat Liney had also gone, joining his home-town club St Mirren for £4,000. After a couple of years there, he went south to Bradford Park Avenue, then Bradford City, where he remained until 1972.

Dundee's grand old man, Gordon Smith, left in February 1964 just short of his 40th birthday. He moved to Republic of Ireland side Drumcondra before retiring at the end of that season after playing just a handful of games for his new club.

That August, Bobby Wishart left Dens, spending short spells at Airdrie and Raith Rovers before retiring in 1965.

In December 1964 came the blow that Dundee fans had long dreaded. Like Ian Ure a year earlier, Alan Gilzean had refused to re-sign. He eventually agreed to sign short-term contracts on the understanding that he would be sold. Sunderland and Italian club Torino had both wanted him, but it was Jimmy Greaves' Tottenham Hotspur who won the race for his signature and paid a new Scottish record fee of £72,500.

Gilzean, who had netted a Dens Park club record of 169 goals in 190 appearances, broke the news to his team-mates during one of their regular lunches at DM

Brown's. He went on to form a devastating partnership with Greaves.

During his time at White Hart Lane he was also part of Spurs' FA Cup-winning side against Chelsea at Wembley in 1967. He gained further winners' medals from two League Cup successes and a UEFA Cup win before retiring in 1974.

By early 1965, Hampden hero Bert Slater was a spent force as young Ally Donaldson began to establish himself as Dundee's top keeper. On his release, Slater joined Watford where he played for four seasons before joining the Vicarage Road coaching staff.

But it was another Scottish goalkeeper who really hit the headlines as it became clear that the dodgy officiating in Milan was sadly not an isolated case of corruption.

That January, a bribery trial resulted in St Mirren goalie Dick Beattie being jailed for nine months for taking payments to 'throw' games.

At the heart of matters was Jimmy Gauld, a Scottish former footballer who had spent most of his career south of the border before gaining a reputation for match fixing. A year earlier, he had sold his story to the *Sunday People* for £7,000, incriminating himself and various other players including Beattie and England internationals Peter Swan and Tony Kay.

Gauld, whose activities were said by the prosecuting counsel to have stretched from Exeter to Dundee, was sentenced to four years in prison. All those convicted were banned from football for life, although some were later allowed to return to the game.

One of the matches cited was Dundee's 5-1 home win over St Mirren before the European Cup semi-final against Milan when Bobby Waddell scored three goals. Later, the Fifer commented, 'That was the only hat-trick I ever scored for Dundee. You certainly didn't think about anything like match fixing when you went out to play. Maybe, though, it was the reason I got these goals but there was nothing to suggest there was anything odd at the time.'

Former team-mates of Beattie were reluctant to condemn him but those at the game recalled him making a number of rash throws out early in the match at Dens.

In 1963/64, Waddell made his mark by averaging a goal in every second game but was unable to win a permanent slot in the side the following season. The signing of Alex Harley to replace the departing Gilzean prompted Waddell to seek a transfer. In March 1965, he was sold to Blackpool, later joining Bradford Park Avenue where he was reunited with Pat Liney. In 1967, Waddell returned to his roots, playing for East Fife before spending a single season with Montrose in 1970/71, before retiring due to injury. The injury woes suffered by Craig Brown had continued and he too moved on, joining Falkirk for £6,000.

In February 1965, Dundee supporters were stunned to hear that manager Bob Shankly had left his office at Dens Park for the last time. Soon afterwards he agreed a five-year deal and record wages to become manager of Hibs to replace Jock Stein, who had taken over at Celtic.

'I'll miss Dens for a while,' he said. 'I'm leaving one good team to start with another and it's always a little sad to leave behind youngsters you have been grooming like Ally Donaldson, Steve Murray, Jocky Scott and George Stewart.'

Many months earlier, Dundee had offered Shankly a similar deal but he never signed it. He was disillusioned by the sale of his top stars. The cup exit at the hands of St Johnstone following the Gilzean transfer was the final straw.

By May, Sammy Kean, whose six-game spell as interim manager until the arrival of new boss Bobby Ancell included a 7-1 win over Hearts at Tynecastle, had also gone. He became manager of Falkirk and would renew his acquaintance with Craig Brown.

That month, Bobby Seith hung up his boots to replace Kean, while there was a shock departure of another of the championship-winning side when Hugh Robertson was allowed to join Dunfermline for £13,000.

Shankly did well in just over four years at Easter Road but found Hibs were every bit as much a selling club as Dundee. Top stars like Neil Martin and Colin Stein were sold. Shankly never did add to that 1962 title triumph. Latterly, he served Stirling Albion both as manager and general manager. A stand at Dens Park now commemorates his achievements at Dundee.

Bobby Seith quickly established a reputation as a top coach, moving on to Rangers as assistant manager to Scot Symon before resigning when he deemed his boss to have been unfairly sacked in late 1967. He prospered as manager at Preston North End and spent a successful four-year spell at Hearts before retiring from the game to take up a new career in chiropody.

Robertson, too, did well at East End Park where he was part of their Scottish Cup-winning side in 1968 and featured in many of their games in Europe. Later, he moved to Arbroath before returning to Dens Park as a coach in the mid-1970s.

In November 1965, the long-serving Alan Cousin was transferred to Hibs for £15,500. Once again he was under the wing of Shankly. After four seasons he joined Falkirk before retiring in 1970.

The World Cup year of 1966 then saw the departure of George Ryden. He had now lost his place to Jim Easton but had finally tasted European football after appearing in the Cup Winners' Cup tie against Zaragoza two years earlier.

Andy Penman was the next to go when Rangers signed him in a part-exchange deal for George McLean following their shock Scottish Cup defeat to Berwick Rangers in 1967.

A year later, Alex Hamilton left for South African football after 11 years with Dundee. He never did get his big move to England. He had, though, been Scotland's first-choice right-back for four years and his 24 international appearances remain a Dens Park record.

The Hamilton–Cox partnership had been one of the most famous in Scotland. Now it was no more.

In April 1969, Cox finally hung up his boots. He spent 13 years at Dens Park. He never gained that elusive international cap but his 433 appearances made him second only to the great Doug Cowie.

Cox and Hamilton renewed their partnership when they later became matchday hospitality hosts at Dens. The former skipper's long-standing commitment to the Dundee cause was honoured when the new Provost Road stand was named after him.

Cox was a veteran of 35 when he hung up his boots. Alex Stuart was seven years younger when he called it a day that same month due to injury. The Aberdonian had captained Bobby Ancell's reshaped side to the 1967 League Cup Final. It was their misfortune to come up against Jock Stein's all-conquering Celtic, who had recently become the first British club to win the European Cup. Dundee lost 5-3 but won many friends with their play and later that season reached the Fairs Cup semi-final before falling to eventual winners Leeds United.

Stuart's retirement left Doug Houston as the sole survivor from the halcyon days of the European Cup, though Ally Donaldson had been a reserve since 1961. Houston was a player of great versatility, moved from being a winger to midfield, then to left-back and central defence. He later become an influential figure as captain and led Dundee to famous UEFA Cup victories over old foes Cologne and AC Milan in 1971. Two years later he left to join Rangers and after a short stay had spells at Dundee United and St Johnstone before several years as part-time manager at Brechin City and Forfar Athletic.

So much for the players and management of that golden era. But what of those involved in the demolition and construction work in the city?

The Tay Road Bridge itself was opened in August 1966 with the event commemorated on the front of Saturday's Dundee versus St Johnstone programme. Construction boss Willie Logan's interest in the welfare of his workers was legendary. He would arrange for the delivery of teatime fish suppers with a Morris Minor van reversing up the temporary carriageway to dish them out, and he provided ice-creams in the summer.

Sadly, Logan was never to see the bridge completed. In January that year, he was killed in an air crash near Inverness airport. He was impatient to return to his base from Edinburgh but, with no suitable Loganair aircraft available, he made the fateful decision to take a charter flight in a Piper Aztec which plunged into a hill west of his destination. Logan's death affected the lives of hundreds of employees and culminated in the liquidation of the Logan Group in 1970.

The new Tay crossing brought a social and economic revolution to the city and north Fife. It opened up communities to business and tourism while making it easier for Fifers to commute. But it marked the end for the Tay ferries, or 'Fifies' as they were better known, just as it had for those in the Forth with the advent of the Forth Bridge in 1964. These sailed from Dundee's Craig Pier to Newport and the final crossings by the *Scotscraig* took place in the shadow of the new bridge ten days before its opening.

Dundee city centre underwent massive change between 1962 and 1973. Many older Dundonians will tell you this was the period when the heart was torn out of the city. The Overgate redevelopment meant the demolition of the historic old Overgate stretching from the corner of Reform Street to North Lindsay Street. It was replaced by the original Overgate shopping centre and the Angus Hotel.

Construction of the Tay Road Bridge came at a cost quite apart from its £6m price tag. It required the demolition of the Royal Arch on Dock Street, where Queen Victoria had entered the city on a visit. Gone too was the adjacent Empress Ballroom. All this was carried out in 1964 and the rubble used as foundations for the approach ramp.

In 1966, Dundee West Railway Station – with its exotic Scottish Baronial style spires – became another casualty of the 'Great Knockin' Doon' to allow the development of the landfall area and inner ring road along Yeaman Shore. The station closed on the same day as the iconic La Scala cinema in Murraygate. Also demolished was Dundee East Station, closed in 1959 but whose strange, half-barrel-shaped edifice still protruded from amidst the cobblestones of East Dock Street.

Arguably, the area of Shore Terrace, behind the Caird Hall and across Dock Street from the Royal Arch, was the living, beating heart of the city. For here was the Dundee Corporation bus station with its ranks of green, double-decker buses amidst a score of 1949-vintage concrete bus shelters.

The nearby arcade was a popular attraction for the youth of the city while the bustling bus terminus itself, accessed by Castle Street and Crichton Street, was the focal point for travellers to all parts of the city and suburbs. It remained, with the view of its Royal Arch and harbour replaced instead by the curves of the Tay Bridge approach ramps. But, by 1973 it too was gone along with the old baths as planners began to modernise the infilled riverside area.

Like many others, former DC Thomson journalist and lifelong Dundee fan Jim Crumley regretted the area's demise and wrote about the changes in 1998.

'In the days when Shore Terrace meant what it said and accommodated the bus station, you could while away the wait between buses watching an endless succession of grubby rustbuckets, dredgers and other river workhorses jostling and toiling on the other side of the street,' he wrote. 'Occasionally a lightship would be hauled in for a paint job.

'And that mysterious little species of railway engine was forever trundling along Dock Street and under the grotesque shadow of the Royal Arch, blackening its skirts with gleeful disrespect, seeing it was supposed to honour a queen.

'All their comings and goings were a part of us, part of the pattern of our sea-smelling street. To this day, more than 30 years after we had it removed from our midst to accommodate the fact that "they" built the road bridge in the wrong place, I still miss it all.'

In 2010, the passing of former Dundee skipper Bobby Cox brought widespread tributes from the football club, former team-mates and supporters alike. Kind words from former Dundee United director Derek Robertson illustrated the great respect in which the team of 1962/63 was held.

He said, 'In the early 60s, it was common for supporters to go to [both] Dens and Tannadice and, although a United fan, I was frequently taken to Dens by my father and uncle and have great memories of Bobby Cox in the European Cup campaign of 1962/63. He brought great credit to the city.'

Sadly, the loss of Cox came just two years before the 50th anniversary of the club's league championship success in 1962.

That title win, their great European run and the goals-galore campaign which saw them finish Scottish Cup runners-up before 120,000 fans at Hampden rightly tend to be rolled up into the club's glory days.

On 28 April 2012, Dundee FC's 50th anniversary championship celebrations were held at the Caird Hall with over 600 in attendance for a special dinner.

High above the City Square were emblazoned the individual names of the men who made history in 1962 and who, along with Bert Slater, proceeded to then put the club, city and Scotland on the European football map.

It was a memorable evening for all in attendance including the surviving members of the 15-man squad, much enhanced by speeches by Ian Ure and Alan Gilzean amongst others. The players themselves talked of their memories of those special days.

'I wouldn't miss this gathering for anything,' said Gilzean. 'Dundee's is still the first result I look for, closely followed by Spurs.'

He rated winning the title with Dundee and reaching the semi-final of the European Cup the following season as major highlights of his career.

Gilzean said, 'Unlike today, it was quite common for teams outside Celtic and Rangers to win the title. Hibs did it a few times when I was growing up after the war. Then Aberdeen, Hearts, ourselves and Kilmarnock. Looking back, Dundee's feat was a bit special.'

Gilzean highlighted the contribution made by Gordon Smith, his hero as a youngster.

'When I was a kid growing up in Coupar Angus, I had a soft spot for Hibs and Gordon was a hero of mine,' he said. 'I was really very happy at Dens and had some great times, but, in 1964, I knew it was time for me to move on. AC Milan offered me £15,000 to stay with Dundee for another year, then sign for them as they already had their full quota of foreign players for the season.

'However, I was determined to move to England as my dream was to play in a cup final at Wembley. Mind you, I thought I would be achieving that in 1963 during our European Cup run as the final was to be played there. Obviously we did far better than anyone expected and but for a bad half-hour in the second half in the San Siro, we might have reached the final against Benfica.'

Gilzean and Ian Ure led the toast at the special dinner to 'absent friends'.

Ure said winning the title was 'the single biggest thing that happened to me in football'.

'I was at my peak physically and it was a great period in my life.

'Playing for Scotland at Wembley was another achievement I was chuffed about but nothing comes close to 1962.

'I am truly grateful for all the good times I had at Dundee. The next season, of course, we went all the way to the European Cup semi-final, and I tell you, we could have won that.

'We were very close but the whole experience was a great reward for winning the league.

'It was a magical time.

'Of all the teams I've played with, Dundee are the one I keep in touch with most.

'I went into football expecting absolutely nothing and thanks to Dundee, look where I ended up.

'They are days I'll never forget.'

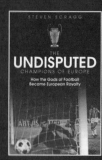

Also available at all good book stores

9781801501125

9781801501149

9781785318276

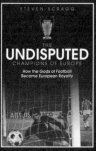

9781801500050

9781785315381

9781785316838

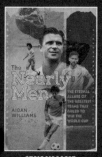

9781801500937

9781801500586

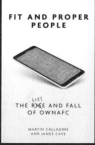

9781801500470